THE AMAZING NELLIE BLY

NELLIE BLY BEFORE HER GLOBE TRIP

THE AMAZING
NELLIE BLY

By

MIGNON RITTENHOUSE

NEW YORK

E. P. Dutton and Company, Inc.

1956

LIBRARY OF CONGRESS CATALOG CARD NUMBER: 56–8324

CONTENTS

LIST OF ILLUSTRATIONS

ILLUSTRATIONS

THE AMAZING NELLIE BLY

CHAPTER I

WHAT GIRLS ARE GOOD FOR

ON A SUMMER DAY in the early 1880's which gave no sign of being eventful, an article called "What Girls Are Good For" appeared in the Pittsburg *Dispatch*. It took a firm stand against the new fad of hiring women to work in offices and shops. A respectable woman, the article said with authority, remained at home until she married. If a husband eluded her, she had two choices left. She might go into teaching or into nursing, provided money for her training could be wangled from a reluctant father. Otherwise, she stayed under his roof or that of a relative and for the remainder of her life accepted the status of houseworker or child's nurse, without the pay.

The article expressed the customary male sentiments of the day, more emphatically than usual because the editors were stirred up over the inroads being made by "those terrible suffragettes," radical females like Susan B. Anthony, openly militant in regard to votes for females, and Elizabeth Cady Stanton, champion of woman's rights, who went striding up and down the country with a following of "bloomer girls." Nobody knew better than the *Dispatch's* managing editor, George A. Madden, that since the Civil War the manpower shortage had increasingly drawn women into mills and factories, but he felt a barricade must be erected against such an alarming trend. Women in politics were unthinkable, as obviously out of place there as they would be in such a masculine stronghold as his own, a newspaper office.

The article received the expected male commendation from Mr. Madden's business associates. He was happily married and his wife, busy with the children, made no comment. Other matters had taken its place in his active editorial mind when a few days later his memory was refreshed. Going through the morning mail, he read one letter and winced. Then he read it again, and a third time, even though it bore no signature, and for a reason. It was a reply to the "What Girls Are Good For" story, and it sizzled. It was a rebuke to the newspaper's old-fashioned attitude, a declaration of independence for woman, a war cry to them to take their proper place in a man's world, to lead interesting, useful, and profitable lives.

The anonymous communication was well written, blazing with conviction. But there was more than that to challenge Mr. Madden's interest. It made sense.

The busy editor finally tossed it into the pile, finished the remainder of the mail, and went back to reading the tissue-paper slips bearing the telegraphic news. But when he had them impaled neatly on the nearby spindle, he took up the letter again. It intrigued him. He studied the handwriting. It appeared feminine, as feminine as the attitude it expressed. But surely no *woman* could write so logically and so eloquently.

He could not publish the thing, even with a signature. It was against his principles, against popular opinion. But he did want to know who had sent it. An idea came to him. He would advertise in the columns of the *Dispatch* for the writer's name and address and, if he obtained them, he might assign a story to be written on the other side of the question. The author would turn out to be a man, of course, perhaps taking this way to attract attention and get a job. Madden would certainly give him one, if he wrote like this consistently.

The advertisement appeared the next day. A reply came almost at once.

The letter had been written by a woman. Her name was Elizabeth Cochrane and she lived in Pittsburg.

George Madden was a newspaperman by both training and instinct; he always followed a hunch. He wrote to Miss Cochrane and asked for an article on "Girls and Their Spheres in Life."

Again she was prompt; the article arrived within a few days. The editor read it and found it good. He paid for it. Then he abandoned caution. Fortifying himself, for he was positive he was opening the door to a battle-ax suffragette, he suggested that Elizabeth Cochrane might like to discuss further work for his paper.

He received no answer to this epistle and was totally un-prepared for what happened next.

It was several days later that the door of the city room

opened and a lady entered. She paused, looking with interest about the cluttered, dirty room, with its battered desks,
its piles of copy paper, its glaring gaslights. She sniffed
delicately its all-pervading odor of printer's ink. Most of
the reporters were in from their runs and at work, but the
activity diminished as one by one the men became aware
of their visitor. From under their hats and over their cigars,
they stared in complete amazement. Few women dared
come here for any reason, but such a one as this had never
before appeared.

"I am looking for Mr. Madden," the visitor said in a soft
voice. Speechless, the men nearest her indicated the managing editor's desk and she made her way to it with a rustle
of skirts. The occupant, aware that activity in the office
suddenly had stopped dead, looked up and saw her there.

"I am Elizabeth Cochrane," the lady informed him.

She was nothing he had imagined. Battle-ax indeed! He
surveyed her with a newsman's eye for descriptive details.

She was a girl, a young girl; she could not yet have
reached eighteen. She was slender and dainty and stood
about five feet five in high-buttoned, size two-and-a-half
shoes. She was modishly dressed in skirt and jacket and
wore a delicate ruching at her neckline. Under a becoming
sailor hat, reddish brown bangs curled over a broad forehead. Her face was oval, her jaw a little too square, but her
mouth was wide and generous. She had hazel eyes, honest
and intelligent and, Mr. Madden guessed, capable of a
twinkle that might match the impishness that lurked in
her expression. But she was very grave now. She gave him

the impression that she knew the men staring at her were muttering, "What is a *lady* doing in a newspaper office?" in the same manner they might ask, "What is a *lady* doing in a saloon?" Her behavior replied simply and directly, "Minding her own business and remembering she is a lady, which should protect her anywhere."

"You sent for me." It was not a question but a statement.

In a sense he had. But in writing her about further work it had not crossed his mind that she would come here unannounced. He had planned an interview soon, in some more appropriate spot. But here she was, and he was in for it.

When not in the office, George Madden prided himself on his manners. They did not fail him now. He rose, took off the derby he always pushed to the back of his head while he worked, and dusted off a chair, which he offered to Miss Cochrane. She settled herself, looking about the office interestedly, and then fixed her gaze on his face. But she left him to continue the conversation. She was smart, this girl. George Madden knew it at once.

"I wrote to you about more of your stories," he said. "Your piece wasn't bad. How'd you like to do a series sometime for the *Dispatch?*"

Her expression was one of mingled astonishment and childish glee.

"Here, do you mean?" she demanded. "Write them here in this office?"

That was too much. Madden backed down fast.

"We will decide that later on, Miss Cochrane." He took

out his handkerchief and wiped his forehead while she waited again. "Have you any idea what you might do for us next?" he got out finally.

"Indeed I have. It's a subject I'm interested in almost as much as spheres for girls."

"What is it?" he asked curiously.

She smiled at him. *The girl had charm.*

"Divorce."

George Madden jumped as though she had stabbed him with the jeweled pin she wore in her hat. Divorce was a subject mentioned in hushed tones and seldom in mixed society. What could this child possibly know about it? She was faking and she had taken him in; he had been on the verge of making a fool of himself. He picked up his great desk shears and began to clip items from the rival newspapers. His manner suggested dismissal.

The girl opposite him flushed, trying not to appear disconcerted. It was clear she had not impressed Mr. Madden as she had hoped to, although she had worn her mother's best hatpin with the real diamond in it. He thought she couldn't handle such a big story. But he had been interested by her letter. He had bought her first article. She wouldn't accept defeat now, not when she really had been inside a newspaper office and when she needed and wanted the work so desperately.

"You wouldn't take a story on that subject?" she asked, trying to keep her voice calm.

"We'd use one, written in the right fashion. But I doubt a girl of your age and experience is much of an authority."

Her relief showed in her face. So that was it. It was not a question of her style, but did she know what she was talking about? She rose, gathering up her skirts with a swish.

"Sorry," mumbled Madden. He hadn't expected her to give up so easily, but since she was that type it was just as well. He struggled out of his chair as Miss Cochrane extended a delicate gloved hand.

"There's nothing to be sorry about, Mr. Madden. Thank you for the pleasant talk. I'll write the article. You can decide when you read it how much I know about divorce."

CHAPTER II

A NAME—A JOB

Elizabeth Cochrane came out of the plain, flat-roofed building of the Pittsburg *Dispatch* and walked rapidly down Fifth Avenue. The editor was right; she had no personal experience at all with divorce. But as far back as she could remember she had heard about her father's legal studies of it and of many other subjects. When she had exhausted a portfolio that had belonged to him she would have to do little additional research. She felt certain that by combining its facts and figures with the life stories told her by women in her lodginghouse she would have an article that was both substantial and moving.

She crossed the street, dodging several carriages, a dray that had been caught in the evening traffic, and a stray dog. A cable car came clanging down the steep grade and she considered boarding it. Then she decided the walk back to her boardinghouse would give her a fine opportunity to think, as well as save her carfare.

A wind began to blow, bearing the foul odors from the smokestacks which lined the three merging rivers of the city. Elizabeth put her handkerchief to her nose and hurried on. She felt a pang of homesickness for the pine-scented air of the Kiskimenta hills. There were many trees there and she knew them all—name, appearance, odor. They had always been part of her life. How quick she had been to leave them! Now she thought almost wistfully of them and the childhood they symbolized, the childhood in Cochran's Mills.

Elizabeth had been born there, in a rambling farmhouse, on May 5, 1867. Her father's name was Michael Cochran. It was Elizabeth herself who, longing for a fancy touch, had added the final *e*. That was after her father, a colorful fellow of Irish descent, had risen from laborer and millworker to millowner, proprietor, postmaster, justice of the peace, and finally Associate Judge of Armstrong County. Gradually he had come to own most of the land in the hamlet and the name of the place had been changed from Pitts Mills to Cochran's Mills.

Elizabeth was the third child of Mr. Cochrane's second marriage. Eventually the family included ten children. There were three brothers of her own and three half brothers. A favorite brother and a sister, as gentle as Elizabeth was spirited, were born after she was. Boys were no problem to the younger girl, but Elizabeth was in competition with them from the first day she walked.

Elizabeth needed spirit. Described as "puny" by neighbors, who prophesied she would not live to grow up, egged on as she was by the boys in the family to new feats of daring, her courage never failed her. The lads, big, muscular, teased and tormented. They did not mean to be unkind, but they challenged her constantly and something in her rose to meet the challenge. Anything they could do, she would do—ride standing up on the old horse as it lumbered across the field; climb to the top of the big apple tree; race a whole troop of children to the one-room log schoolhouse —she never refused. Often she stumbled and fell, bruised her knobby knees, or grew so breathless the world spun around her. But she never gave up. Her appearance remained delicate, almost doll-like. But she had a fierce independence and a fighting spirit, a resolution to "stand up to the boys."

She developed a kind of dual personality. Her mother, a tiny woman, gentle and fastidious, wanted Elizabeth to have the same qualities. She also wanted to emphasize the little girl's delicate complexion. She made her dainty dresses of pink gingham, which resulted in the child's father nicknaming her "Pinky." The boys called her "Lizzie" to tease her. She loved one name as much as she hated the other.

When the family moved a short distance to the small mining town of Apollo, life was pleasant but different. Then Mr. Cochrane died. It was a tragic blow. But his widow kept his memory alive, talking about him constantly and giving the children his books and papers to read. Elizabeth especially found them interesting and she thought of him always with affection and respect. He became to her a dream image of the perfect husband, father, and companion.

Elizabeth was "Pinky" to the school crowd. She swam in the river with them, and went sleigh-riding over the steep hills. She was popular, and full of fun. But her thoughts were not confined by city limits. Her favorite pastime was to go alone to the small red brick station and watch the one-a-day train to Pittsburg puff past. She dreamed of travel, of adventure.

She made stories about it. Her teachers thought Pinky saucy and precocious, but were intrigued by her literary efforts. These had to do with haunted castles and knights in armor and stupendous feats of daring. Usually the heroine was a girl who looked like Elizabeth and who emerged victorious not only against dragons and super-natural beings but against the scoffing opposition of the entire male sex. Constant conflict with six brothers was showing its results.

But she was busy and happy, a small town belle, until the older children went away. Then Pinky went off too, to boarding school for a time, but that was cut short by ill health. So instead she buried herself in the library at home and began to write stories in earnest. She tried all kinds and searched for material in everything she could lay her hands on, law books and records of her father's, theology, romantic novels.

There was a big square piano in the room. She practiced on it and studied French and German. When she couldn't stand the house, she rode horseback.

But finally she could bear it no longer. Her sisters married, her brothers were in business in Pittsburg. Pinky, popular with the young men of Apollo, had no desire to settle down there. Mrs. Cochrane was reluctant to leave, but her husband's seventeen-thousand-dollar estate, once real wealth, had melted away. It would be pleasant to be near her sons. She let Elizabeth persuade her to move to Pittsburg, where, Pinky informed her, she would earn their living as a writer. She had no intention of scraping along on relatives' doles, even if that was the accepted custom for girls in her position.

On the basis of her expectations, they lived at first in the fashionable sections of the city. Then, week by week, they moved down, finding cheaper and cheaper lodginghouses, until their fellow roomers were workers in shops and factories, weary, workworn, and underpaid.

These women emphasized what Elizabeth herself was learning from bitter experience, how next to impossible it was for a poor woman alone in the world to keep her independence and self-respect. She wrote constantly for every market she could discover, stories, articles, lurid romances. Many of them she destroyed as not good enough; others were rejected or brought almost nothing. Her own experiences in job seeking were similar to those of the shopgirls. She found few openings, long hours, hard work, and not enough pay to live on.

The article "What Girls Are Good For" had been the spark that had caused the explosion. Elizabeth had written her letter in the white heat of indignation. It was her personal cry of protest, her personal bill of rights. She never dreamed the paper would inquire who was the author. The advertisement made her gasp when she saw it and, when her answering letter brought her an assignment, she was wild with excitement. Had her chance come at last? She felt it had. She had written at top speed and almost cried over her first "big" money.

The plan of going directly to the office to reply in person to Mr. Madden's query had been a daring one. But she had been sure, in the way she had been sure long ago when the boys had challenged her to a stunt seemingly impossible. More articles, the editor had written. She must make certain of as many as possible.

The idea of a regular job made her dizzy. Of course, Mr. Madden had pulled it away again almost at once, looking skeptical about even the next story. What did she know about divorce? She would show him.

But, as she came down the street toward the dingy house where she and her mother were "temporarily" lodging, her assurance faded. The door, its peeling paint a bilious green, the sagging baby carriage on the porch, the dirty hallway, the high, strained voices of the women in the ugly parlor—all suddenly made her fearful for her own future. Broken families, broken homes, broken lives, broken hearts—such things should not be!

She started up the stairs, forcing herself to be impersonal, to think of them only in terms of her article. Divorce! Suddenly she knew what she would stress. The divided family, divided by sickness, poverty, indifference, or death.

Among her father's papers there was a bundle of documents he had collected for the study he had once made on the alarming increase in the divorce rate in America. Elizabeth had always felt his books and papers were a legacy to her. With that to guide her and what her heart knew, she would tell the story.

"Pinky," she heard her mother's voice call. Mrs. Cochrane stood in the doorway of her room, looking anxious. Elizabeth stooped and kissed her.

"It's all right, Mother. The editor and I got along fine. But I can't stop to talk now. I've got a job to do."

It was daylight when she finished. Her fingers were smudged and cramped, her back ached, and when she looked into the mirror as she brushed her hair she saw there were deep circles under her eyes. But the article was written. She rested for a couple of hours, then dressed and took it to the *Dispatch* office. She placed it on Mr. Madden's desk and would have fled, but he called to her and she went back and sat rigidly while he read it.

All her pride in what she had done oozed out as she waited. Why hadn't he let her go and simply sent her a note of refusal? By the time he had turned the last page, she was convinced she had written trash.

But Mr. Madden didn't think so. The piece was human and it was sound and it was challenging, he said. If the public reacted to it as he believed they would, it could be the first of a series.

And he would go even further. He paused, looking at this young girl, aware he was about to do a thing unprecedented in the annals of Pittsburg journalism. Then he told Elizabeth Cochrane that if the divorce series caught on with *Dispatch* readers he would give her a job on the staff. *And he would pay her five dollars a week.*

Courtesy of Carnegie Library, Pittsburgh, Pennsylvania

Fifth Street, Pittsburg, on which street the Pittsburg *Dispatch* was located.

It was a fortune. He found the expression on her face a very touching one.

"Of course, you'll have to be worth it," he added. "Think you can be?"

"Yes, I do," said Elizabeth stoutly. "I've got ideas. Ideas are worth money."

They were. And she had them. There was no doubt of it. The editor took a deep breath for one final matter. It was most unusual for a woman's name to appear on newspaper articles. There was a special problem in this matter of divorce. It would be best if Miss Cochrane used an assumed name—a pen name. He suggested some fine-sounding ones: Archibald Blake—Reginald Hammond. . . .

Elizabeth shook her head. But her eyes twinkled. She would certainly use a pen name if he preferred, she said reasonably. But not a man's name.

"What do you want to be called, then?" Madden's tone was a little sharp. She knew she had to produce her nom de plume quickly.

His assistant, Erasmus Wilson, was humming to himself. It was a Stephen Foster song, one of the most popular by the Pittsburg composer—

> Heigh, Nelly, ho! Nelly, listen lub to me,
> I'll sing for you, play for you, a dulcem melody. . . .

She did not wait for him to finish. She knew the rest. Mr. Madden knew it too. "Nelly Bly, Nelly Bly, bring de broom along," he sang.

Nelly, decided Elizabeth. No—Nellie; *Nellie Bly*. A good

name for a girl reporter who went through fire and flood and into the jaws of death to bring back her story.

She was dreaming again. She brought herself up sharply. She didn't need to dream any more. The chance was here. But who was to tell her that one day Nellie Bly's realities would far surpass the girlish longings of Elizabeth Cochrane?

The articles on divorce were a success and the name of the mysterious person who wrote them came to be almost as much discussed as they were. Who was she? Was she *really* a woman, or some male reporter using the name for disguise? If she was a female, she must be elderly, for her point of view was mature. Still, she was full of fire and her writing was charged with youthful exuberance.

By the time the series was finished, Pittsburg readers were agog. Nellie Bly was the subject of constant speculation. Women gossiped as they sewed. Businessmen argued at lunch. Police dragged off to jail a couple of inebriated gentlemen, still contending: "She's a woman!" "Naw, I tell you a man uses the name and writes the stuff." The mystery was part of the game and the *Dispatch* played it up fully.

But while the readers wondered, the young reporter went about her business. The series finished, she wrote scattered articles, and she was always on the search for new subjects. The problems of the working woman had come into the divorce stories; their lot was something in which she was deeply interested. She began to frequent not only the boardinghouse district but the very poorest sections of the city. At first her appearance caused a near riot there. Boys hooted at her, women sneered, men made remarks. But Nellie kept her dignity and her purpose. And eventually she made friends. And with friends she could frankly discuss their problems. But she did not mention her purpose in the office until one morning when she approached the managing editor with the type of "unprecedented" idea she had learned he would appreciate.

She had become fast friends with George Madden. He himself had come up the rugged way. As a boy he had worked in a printing office secretly while supposedly attending school. He had come to Pittsburg from Canada to take a job in a composing room and had gone through the routines of reporter, copy-desk man, and telegraph editor before he attained his present position. He was tense, nervous, a prodigious worker, and his friends were always predicting a breakdown for him. Instead he thrived. Right now he was on top of the world. Against all caution he had engaged a female, *a girl* to work on the *Dispatch*, and she was building circulation.

But he hesitated a little when she put her plan before him.

"The slums in Pittsburg are among the worst in the world," she told him earnestly. "Why should they be? Why should there be slums anywhere? I think it is because most people don't know, any more than they know about the awful conditions in factories, the way girls work from day-

light to dark in filthy unsanitary places, for hardly enough
to keep them alive. If people learn, maybe they will change
things."

"What's your campaign?"

"To show them the truth. To tell the facts about the
immigrants we get over here and then don't take care of.
Welsh, Irish, Scotch—good people who'll make good citizens. But they're jammed in, frightened, unassimilated."

"After you've said it, what then?"

"I want to make the government and the citizens of
Pittsburg face up to what is going on in this city. I want
to go into streets where buildings are firetraps and the
halls full of garbage and rats; into factories where women
do piecework, without heat and in dim light; into lofts
where children who look like skeletons begin to earn almost
as soon as they can walk. I want to tell the public about
these things and I want to show them. I'd like to take an
artist with me, and bring you pictures of what life is like
for thousands in this city that's so proud of itself."

It was a long speech. She was breathless. But she'd said it.

A crusade. And a good one, thought Madden. It would
strike snags—there would be big interests who would not
like to have the public learn the facts about their slum
property. But the *Dispatch* had never been timid. And the
people of Pittsburg were entitled to the truth. This might
be the first step in pushing for a lot of reform. He had found
out already that this girl was not only a good reporter, she
was a born leader. Give her a cause, appeal to her sympathies for the downtrodden, and she went into battle. So

29

Madden said yes because he couldn't possibly say no. And the next day Nellie Bly was off with her artist to get material for her "real experience" stories.

Madden was not without uneasiness, however. Editorials appeared constantly in his paper, as in other Pittsburg journals, pointing out the increasing danger to life in the smoky city. He read one scowling:

"A man's life is not safe on some of our streets, even in broad daylight. After nightfall a respectable woman, unaccompanied by an escort, can scarcely leave her doorway without insult."

He cautioned Nellie. She laughed at him. If women were not safe on the streets on respectable business, it was high time they became so. She intended to set the fashion.

The working woman stories were an even greater success than the divorce articles, for they were the stuff of life—the tragedy of a family of twelve in a heatless room, of women old long before their time, of children little better than slaves—people without help and without hope. Nellie wrote about them until every right-minded citizen in Pittsburg felt their salvation as a personal obligation. There was agitation; there were public mass meetings. And Nellie interviewed those responsible for the conditions as well as the victims of them. With a passionate honesty she tried the case of the suffering in Pittsburg in the court of public opinion. And nobody in the docket wanted to be found guilty.

Letters poured into the *Dispatch* office: letters from

THE HOUSE WHERE NELLIE WAS BORN—COCHRAN'S MILLS, ARMSTRONG COUNTY, PENNSYLVANIA

THE YOUNG NELLIE BLY—
ELIZABETH COCHRANE

NELLIE BLY AFTER HER GLOBE TRIP

businessmen, from the clergy, from suffragettes, and from plain people. But the letters Nellie put away to treasure were those from the poor of Pittsburg who had found in her a friend and champion.

CHAPTER III

GIRL REPORTER

THE "poor working girl" assignment was soon finished. But Nellie Bly was just beginning.

Before long she knew every winding hilly road in the city of Pittsburg and had traveled a distance equivalent to a transcontinental journey on its horse-drawn stages or cable cars. She had tramped for miles through its least known sections. She had the cooperation of the city's officials and was considered a pal by the police. Of the many friends she had made, she was closest to the mighty and the poor.

The general public still speculated about her, but she strove to preserve her anonymity. It was best not to be recognized when she had investigating to do. But, if her face was not known, her name was. It was heard constantly around the city. Subscribers sent letters about her to the editor and mashers wrote notes to Nellie Bly.

In the office the men had accepted her, silken petti-coats and all—her ability and vivacity had won them —and had shortened her name to Nell. Mr. Madden raised her salary from five to fifteen dollars a week, and besides writing her own feature stories she "covered" news for several departments, attending society weddings, lantern-slide lectures, art exhibits, and church services. She was invited to join the newly formed Pittsburg Press Club, a signal honor indeed for a *female*, and this in spite of the fact she had scooped the city's best reporters on several stories. She wrote interviews with celebrities: Andrew Carnegie, who advised her always to save part of her income if she wished to succeed in the world; and James Whitcomb Riley, the Hoosier poet, in whose opinion she would succeed in the world only if she spent enough of her money for smart clothes.

She enjoyed it all. She lived in an atmosphere of exciting change. It was an era of new discoveries in many fields; men were finding ways of making life better for everyone.

There was the telephone, first shown at the Centennial Exposition in Philadelphia in 1876 when Nellie was nine years old, now coming into general use. Alexander Graham Bell, a young teacher of deaf children, had invented it in an effort to help his students to hear. The Centennial judges had brushed it aside as a toy until the Emperor of Brazil, visiting the exhibit, picked it up and exclaimed, *"Why, it talks!"* There was wireless, now becoming indispensable in newspaper offices, and the transcontinental railway, laid through Indian country in spite of the menace of scalping knives, bringing the East and West closer together in knowledge and inspiration. There was progress of every kind in the air.

The world had become Nell's pumpkin. And she was not yet nineteen.

33

It was unbelievable that in this short space of time Pittsburg should come to seem confining to her. Not that the city was small; its sprawling area made some assignments in winter very difficult to cover. But suddenly she wanted change, she wanted to see something different. Her passion to travel had never altered since the Apollo days when her goal had been Pittsburg. Now it was some place beyond she longed for, a broader horizon she sought.

One day, sloshing back to the office in the cold rain, she saw a picture of Aztec ruins in a window of an art gallery, and suddenly the answer came to her. *Mexico!* Strange, romantic, full of news stories, it was the ideal spot. She would survey the land and the new government. The *Dispatch* would tell its readers the truth about the mysterious country across the border, for Nellie Bly would write it.

She was so excited by her thoughts that she began to run, her umbrella bobbing up and down with each step. Pedestrians glanced curiously at her billowing skirts and flying veil; the driver of a cable car clanged in salute. But Nellie was oblivious. What a wonderful idea! Mr. Madden *must* let her go. She couldn't wait to ask him.

But when she reached the city room it was deserted except for Erasmus Wilson, the editor's able assistant. He and Nellie had become great friends in spite of Madden's humorously warning introduction of him as "Pittsburg's most eligible bachelor and the world's greatest authority on kissing." He had not tried kissing her yet, but he had given her friendship and advice. He was sixteen years her senior, but she did not mind that at all. In fact, she found she was more attracted to older men than to youthful beaux. Maybe it was because she had loved her father so much, she thought sometimes; she had built his memory into her ideal man. Or maybe she resented male youths who reminded her in any way of her teasing stepbrothers. Elizabeth might have become Nellie, but she still had a great many of Pinky's childhood reactions.

Erasmus waved fraternally to her as she entered and hung up her wet mackintosh and planted her dripping umbrella in a stand she had brought from home. As she went to her desk she coughed a little from her exertions and the impish look came to her eyes. She really ought to get out of this climate; Mr. Madden would see that clearly. But until he arrived she must do some work. She took paper and dipped her pen and began to write the day's stories. But they went badly. Her mind was not on them.

At a second fit of coughing Erasmus Wilson came to her desk. He carried a bottle and spoon.

"Ole Doc Wilson says you need something for that. You don't take care of yourself, Nell."

She gulped the stuff down obediently. A Don Juan bringing her cough syrup. It was funny. He couldn't suspect she coughed for a reason.

But she hadn't fooled him much.

"What's on your mind?" Wilson asked. "You came in here starry-eyed about something."

Nell nodded. "Yes, I did."

35

"Name the great adventure now."

She surveyed him thoughtfully. "If I tell you, will you help me? Persuade Mr. Madden to let me go?"

"Go where?"

She took the plunge. "I want to go to Mexico."

Wilson whistled softly. "The sunny land of the gods, eh? Let me tell you, there's another side to it."

"A bad side?"

"A hidden one Americans don't understand. Joaquin Miller is there right now, writing about it. He has had some startling things to say."

"Joaquin Miller, the Western poet? I hope he stays until I get there. I'd like to know him. I want to know all there is about the country too, the romance, the adventure——"

"Escape. That's all you're seeking, Nell. And so young, too."

"Maybe," she admitted frankly. "Anyhow, there are certain things I'm going to do, Erasmus. Live a free life; be a person, not just a woman. It could be a struggle to do that, if I looked at it that way. But I won't. It can be an adventure and I'm going to make it one."

"You've cut out quite a job for yourself," Erasmus said after a pause. He put a hand on her shoulder. "You're a strange child, younger and freer and yet in some ways wiser than anyone I've ever known. I think you'll make out, even in Mexico."

He took up his bottle and spoon. "You're right. Don't lose the things God gave you as a birthright, no matter what comes."

But George Madden was not so easily persuaded. When she first broached the subject of the trip to him, he only snorted. It was bad enough for her to roam all over Pittsburg unescorted. Mexico was a thousand times worse. No place for a young girl. Even the government there was highly unstable. She might have all sorts of horrible experiences. She might not come out alive.

"But if I do," said Nellie, her eyes shining, "think of the stories I'll bring you."

Mr. Madden thought of them.

Nell's stories, he knew, would be eyewitness accounts of what was going on across the border. Most Americans were under the impression that everything had been moving smoothly since the Emperor Maximilian had been executed in 1867 and the Mexicans, headed by the full-blooded Indian Juarez, had inaugurated a new order. But the ears of trained editors detected rumblings from the neighbor country which did not sound reassuring, and the cheerful stories they received through the Mexican press failed to impress them. Nell had a talent for probing and finding the truth in forbidden places. Still, Mr. Madden felt he must discourage her. She might well get across the border and vanish, as several Americans had done.

She could not go, he said. Unchaperoned, anything might happen. The Mexicans could not understand such conduct.

"I'll take a chaperone, if it's necessary. I'll take Mother."

The little lady would add respectability, certainly, but scarcely provide physical protection. He still said no.

"How would you finance such a trip?" he asked. "It won't be cheap."

"Certainly the *Dispatch* can give me an expense account. I'll send you some special news. It will build circulation, Mr. Madden," she tempted.

The witch. He knew it would. He shouldn't risk her life. It was scandalous, a young girl traipsing off. . . .

"You win," said George Madden.

CHAPTER IV

MEXICO

FOR three days Nellie and her mother sat on the observation platform of the train as it sped across the country. They saw mountains and valleys and snow-covered fields and finally the bright plains of the West. But what went on there shocked them.

"I saw gaunt, tired women plowing the fields, while their lords and masters sat on the fences and smoked," Nellie wrote back. "Farther south there were no fences, so no lazy male ornaments."

It was the middle of the night when the two women, tired and covered with train soot, arrived in El Paso. Nellie's experience with railway stations had been limited to her one arrival and departure from Pittsburg and she was not sure what to do. Trainmen were running along the railroad platform with lanterns, but no one paid any attention to the drowsy passengers. Nellie saw no cabs, not even a Mexican with a wheelbarrow who might trundle their bags to a hotel for them. It was almost the first occasion on which she had wished for a man to take charge. But she dismissed the thought quickly and steered her mother toward the waiting room. There would be shelter there at least, and the ticket agent could give them hotel information.

But the ticket window was closed. The room, dimly lighted by a smoking oil lamp, held men, women, children, and baggage seemingly dumped in one large mass. Some of the men were drinking, some were snoring loudly. The babies cried and the women screamed at them. A group of derelicts passed a bottle of whisky from hand to hand and played poker with greasy cards. The two Cochranes turned back into the darkness.

A man with a lantern passed and Nell called to him and asked about a hotel. His English was broken but she made out that all the hotels were closed at this hour.

"But our train doesn't go until tomorrow afternoon," she protested. "We've got to get some rest."

Again she struggled to understand him as he explained that he had a house, a very good house. He would rent the senorita a room there, a very good room, very cheap.

Cheap or expensive, good or bad, it would be a place to lie down. They followed him, stumbling along the sandy streets to the Mexican section of the town. The room was a cubbyhole, the light a candle, the bed stuffed with straw. They fell upon it, too tired to do more than take off their high button shoes.

The morning was better. And the next evening they were on their way to Mexico.

With every mile they traveled, Nellie's interest in this primitive country increased and her mother's diminished.

The food made Mrs. Cochrane ill, while Nell throve on a diet of beans and cayenne pepper. Nell liked the people, but Mrs. Cochrane was shocked by the naked Indian children. She saw no adventure in having bandits ride after their train. She shivered as an Indian eyed their suitcases covetously. When they finally arrived in Mexico City, she looked it over with more haste than enthusiasm and permitted her daughter to put her on a train for home.

"Tell Mr. Madden I'll be fine. And I'll be sending him lots of stories. And stop worrying, all of you," Nell ordered her affectionately as she kissed her good-by. "I'll be home soon."

But it was six months before Pittsburg saw Nellie Bly again.

She set up her headquarters in Mexico City and there, as in the surrounding country, she found sharp contrasts. The rich ruled. Dressed in the latest Paris fashions, they went to bullfights and the theater and had every luxury. The men wore silk hats and swung "nobby" canes; the gentlewomen covered their faces with a heavy coating of powder. Both men and women wore French opera heels. For Nell, accustomed to the sedate styles of Pittsburg, it was like a pageant to see fine ladies riding horseback along the boulevards, clad in bright habits adorned with gold and silver buttons, broad sombreros on their elaborately coiffeured heads.

But everywhere too she saw the masses of the poor. They sat in the shadows of statues and cathedrals, these peons whose lands had been taken from them by their masters.

As she walked along the streets at night she saw dark groups huddled together which turned out to be whole families gone to bed.

"They never repose," she wrote home, "but sit with heads on their knees. When they are hungry they eat what they have scraped together during the day; spoiled meat and scraps boiled over a handful of charcoal."

At best they had only huts for shelter and straw mats for beds. But beneath their dirt and ignorance Nell found goodness and compassion. A man passed bearing a coffin on his head and all the men about her stood bareheaded as long as he was in sight. She talked with a homeless boy who was carefully carrying his baby brother on his back.

"As a people," she wrote, "they do not seem malicious, quarrelsome, unkind, or evilly disposed. Yet most of them live and die homeless, poor, uncared for, untaught. *They are worse off by thousands of times than were the slaves in the United States.*"

The old question rang in her ears again. Why? *Why?*

But it took months of danger and disenchantment to make Nellie Bly turn home. She made a deal with a president of three Mexican railroads and traveled about the country on passes. She went everywhere unescorted and saw all there was to see. In countless skirmishes, swarthy innkeepers found to their astonishment they could not cheat this baby-faced *gringo*. She picked up a knowledge of both pure Spanish and the Mexican version and got to know people of every degree. She stayed in wayside huts and in some of the finest homes, investigated palaces and dank prisons, sent back detailed reports of Americans who had vanished over the border and now existed on rations given them only twice a week. The lucky ones, she told her readers, were those who were "shot in the back for trying to escape."

As she had hoped, she met Joaquin Miller, pursuing investigations of his own. He dubbed her "Little Nell, a second Columbus" for her daring. But none of it seemed daring to her. It was all in line of duty.

Miller took her to Tacubaya, once the home of Montezuma's favorite chief, now a fabulous gambling resort, with tables piled high with gold and silver. Even her experienced companion was astonished. "It's old California," he kept repeating, "with the roughness left out." It was very gay. Many fireworks were set off and women in picturesque costumes sang the country's popular song, "I am pure Mexican; no Spanish blood in me."

The children were entranced by Nell's costumes and so, she noticed, were the men. There were many balls and picnics and bullfights to which she was invited, and there were ardent protestations of love to boot from her Mexican suitors. She was showered with flowers and notes. She laughed and tore up most of the letters, but kept one for a souvenir.

"Dear Entrancing Angel," it read. "Your loving slave has been made to feel the bliss of Heaven by your gracious condescension to notice his maddening devotion to you. I long to touch your exquisite hand that I may be made to realize my happiness is earthly. Bless me with a smile and I am forever your most devoted, who lives only to promote your happiness. . . ."

Nell found it all amusing. But she preferred American men. She cut short the social affairs and got on with her sightseeing.

She went to many out-of-the-way places never before visited by foreigners. She stayed in small villages, each with its own army, and saw the soldiers—half-breeds, Indians, and old convicts—smoking marijuana cigarettes. She reported this too to Pittsburg.

"One cigaro is made, and the men, sitting in a ring, partake of it in turn. One man takes a draw and blows the smoke into the mouth of the nearest man. In turn he gives it to the next one and so on around the circle. One cigarette will intoxicate the lot for as long as five days."

When she visited the village of Dordola, high in the mountains, where there had been a colony of Americans under Maximilian, she found all had been executed but one, the doctor, too useful to be discarded.

"Mexico had it the best under Maximilian," he said. "Juarez was good in some ways, but he sowed the seeds of discontent by corrupting the churches and organizing national lotteries. Those who came after each went him one better. But some day Mexico will throw off this yoke of ignorance and become a true republic. Some day there will be equal opportunities not only in America but in all the world."

Nellie hoped he was right. There was much here discouraging, but much to work for, too. She wanted to have a part in the reform, and she might have stayed on, but she lost her head. She was well aware that Article Thirty-three of Mexico's Constitution warned the "pernicious foreigner" not to speak or write too freely of this land and its inhabitants. In her reports she had avoided politics and she had sprinkled praise of the country through them. She had tried to withhold severely critical remarks, as there would be opportunity to publish them after she got home. However, one day in hot indignation over some new injustices she threw discretion to the winds and spoke her mind.

"Mexico is a republic in name only," she began an exposé written for the *Dispatch*. "It is the worst monarchy in existence. An organized ring allows one member to say who shall be President. The government-controlled National lottery permitted Señor Gonzales, former President, to rake in $26,220,000 in four years of official life. President Porfirio Diaz has two years from December to serve, providing a revolution does not cut his term short. Mexican papers never publish a word against the government or officials. People dare not breathe a word against them. Editors are thrown into prison for even hinting the government needs improvement."

Her angry story was widely copied in the States. It was not long before an American newspaper containing it made its way back to the government-controlled Mexican press. A few days later Nell found an envelope slipped under the door of her hotel room. It contained a clipping from a Mexico City journal, condemning her severely for making such charges. On its margin were scribbled in Spanish these words:

"Nellie Bly, one button is enough."

She knew it was a warning. She would be permitted to send no more stories from Mexico. Her visit might as well end.

But, though she was forced to leave, she did not intend to discard the product of all her investigation. Her suitcase was crammed with notes on the country, and she determined to take them with her. If the authorities saw them, they might have her shot "while trying to escape," as they had other Americans. But it seemed a risk she must take. She had struck only one verbal blow; they might not realize she had supplies for a series of them.

She observed from the day the note arrived that she was being watched by the "secret police." Their methods were not exactly subtle; a group of them followed her wherever she went. She decided that if she could not lose them she would use them and went ahead with her preparations. She bought a ticket to El Paso, purchased a stunning Paris dress and chapeau, and then made a great show of shopping for Mexican souvenirs and gaudy lingerie. When the day came to leave, she put on the new outfit and her most demure expression, took her suitcase in her hand, and walked out of her hotel.

As she expected, several members of the police lounged on the corner; when she summoned a hansom cab they rapidly closed in on her. Her hands felt cold and her heart thumped hard. But as they approached her she turned to them with an expression of happy relief. She picked out the leader, a handsome swaggerer, and looked up at him with appealing hazel eyes.

"Señor, you and your companions appear to be gallant gentlemen. What fortune for me you are here! You see how heavy my bag is? It is loaded with the gifts I have bought in your beautiful Mexico for my friends at home. They are very *personal* gifts—for ladies." She managed a blush. "Señor, it is proper for a girl to travel alone in the States. But I learn that is not etiquette here. Will you show me how to get on the train with my presents, so I make no mistakes?"

She looked as guileless as a child; the Paris gown was chic. Whether it was the expression, the costume, or the speech she did not know, but the result was better than Nell had dared hope for. The men pressed forward, beaming at her. But it was the leader himself who gained possession of the bag. He offered her his arm with a flourish.

"I will take charge of this little matter," he informed the others. "You may go about your duties." While they sulked, he helped Nell into the cab and seated himself beside her. She chattered on about her purchases, but he gave no sign he had stood outside each shop while she made them. His admiring gaze indicated only sympathy for a pretty señorita in distress. At the station he found her train, placed her in her seat. But when she reached for her suitcase he handed it to the conductor.

"The señorita is the niece of President Diaz," he said impressively. "She is to be treated with every consideration. She carries many gifts to friends in the States. Take personal charge of her bag for her. It is not to be searched, you will understand."

"*Si. Si.*" The conductor, visibly impressed, went off with it. Nellie's escort took her hand.

"A pleasant journey, *and a safe one,* Señorita," he said. Then he bowed low and kissed her fingers. She watched him swagger off down the platform. His back told her nothing.

Had her ruse actually succeeded? Or was this a trap, with the conductor even now searching her baggage and the police waiting in the next car? It seemed an eternity to Nell before the train began to move. But, tense and anxious as she was, she closed her eyes and when the conductor came near her she pretended to doze. He loaded her with the attentions suitable to the President's niece. But not until they reached El Paso did he restore her suitcase.

Nellie knew then she was safe. But what of her material? Had they confiscated it or were her precious papers still there? She rushed into the El Paso station and lifted the lid to her bag. Nothing appeared to have been touched. The "luxuries" for her friends, undisturbed, still covered material for dozens of stories which would tell the truth about Mexico. These were the real gifts she carried. George Madden would be grateful for them.

CHAPTER V

THE GREAT JOSEPH PULITZER

THE MEXICAN trip, undertaken so lightheartedly, proved to be an important turning point in Nellie Bly's career. She had gone off on it an amateur, a girl familiar with but one section of her own country. She returned a seasoned traveler, with first-hand knowledge of customs, politics, and people of another land. Her smattering of foreign language had expanded to include a usable vocabulary in Spanish. She now considered herself an experienced reporter, and no country and no assignment seemed beyond her.

When she found the extent to which her stories had been copied from the *Dispatch* and her regional reputation had grown, the thought was inevitable that the time had come to find new newspaper offices to conquer, to turn toward the mecca of all writers, New York. Again she sought the counsel of Erasmus Wilson.

"I've got a bag full of feature material that's perfect for a syndicate," she told him. "And I've got a Paris hat and dress and sixty-five dollars I saved out of my expense money. Won't that do for a start?"

"You've got a nice tan, too," he observed, admiring the bronzed effect produced by the Mexican sun. "But New York's a big, bad town."

Nellie laughed.

"Pittsburg's still no churchyard, in spite of our cleanup campaign and the *Dispatch* editorials. Do we have to go over all that again. You made scary remarks about Mexico too. Remember?"

"Mexico was a trip. But if you go to New York you probably won't come back here, Nellie. You might miss the friends you've made in Pittsburg," he added significantly.

"Of course I'll miss them. But I'll make friends in New York, too. Encourage me, Erasmus. I came home from Mexico safe and sound, didn't I?"

"Luckily you did."

"I'm always lucky. And I'm older now," Nellie reminded him.

Erasmus Wilson surveyed her glumly. She was almost twenty. But he was thirty-six. The difference in their ages did not diminish with time. He sighed. The girl must have her chance. He had felt from the beginning she was destined for spectacular success. He would not stand in her way. He need not imagine he could, he admitted with candid self-appraisal.

"What is it you really want out of life?" he asked her curiously. "And don't give me generalities like success, riches, and romance. Be specific."

"I'll try to be," she agreed. She spoke thoughtfully. "I want to write. And I want my writing to make the world

50

better for lots of people. I want to work and I want to do it as an individual, and not be treated as if I weren't up to a real job because I'm a woman. I like being feminine, though —pretty clothes, parties, beaux." She considered. "I want money, enough to let me do the things important to me, like traveling. I want friends. . . ."

"And marriage? Where's the Prince in this tale?"

"I guess I want him too, someday." She laughed. "After I've done the rest, it could be fun to fall in love."

"Crash a New York paper, reform the world, fall in love, and marry a millionaire! There's a modest set of ambitions for you. But, if anybody can achieve them, you will. I hope you get the lot, Nell."

Nell laughed.

But while wealth, love, and marriage were still rosy dreams, the desire to crash a New York newspaper office grew stronger day by day. Finally Nell knew she had to try it. In the summer of 1887 she headed for the big town, excited, a little afraid, but determined. She had arranged to sell some of her Mexican material there. It would give her a small income, and with her nest egg she was sure she could manage until she could establish herself.

She rented a furnished room, unpacked her Mexican notes and her few belongings, and set out to get a line on the metropolis.

The hub of the New York newspaper world, in that year and for many years to come, was Park Row. Here was the home of that distinguished journal, the New York *Times,* of the lusty *Herald,* of Greeley's famous *Tribune,* of Dana's puckish *Sun.* And here, in an ordinary-looking building at numbers 31 and 32, was that blazing new meteor among American newspapers, Pulitzer's *World.*

Joseph Pulitzer, a penniless lad from Budapest, had been brought by agents from Hungary to America to serve in the Union Cavalry during the Civil War. When the shooting was over, he had found what jobs he could in St. Louis, had been mule driver, freight handler, and cabin boy on a steamship operating between St. Louis and Memphis. He had worked in a print shop, fought his way to a reporting job on a German newspaper, and then in an incredibly short time had become the publisher of the most prosperous newspaper in St. Louis, the *Post-Dispatch.*

But when a political shooting had involved his managing editor, Colonel John A. Cockerill, he had sold the sheet, and his great current project was his bouncing boisterous new journal in the East. When he had bought the down-at-the-heel *World* from financial wizard Jay Gould in May, 1883, everybody, including Gould himself, had said the date marked Pulitzer's debut as a prize sucker. Everybody, that was, except Pulitzer. A frail man, his mind and methods were those of a giant. In his characteristically tempestuous manner he'd quickly turned what appeared to be a dying newspaper into a vital and successful one.

By the time Nellie Bly arrived in New York, publishers all over America were looking to the *World* for the much talked of "new direction." The paper not only had the biggest scoops; it had principles. Reform was its watchword. Corruption at home and abroad was unconditionally attacked in its columns. It was more than a news journal; it was a power, its pioneering, unorthodox methods irresistible.

To Nellie the *World* was a magnet. She spent her first stifling summer days working for a small syndicate which had contracted for her Mexican material. But she spent her evenings dreaming up methods to storm the Pulitzer portals.

In addition to the attraction of its policy, the *World* had another feature which appealed to Nellie Bly. She had reconnoitered carefully and found that there was no reception room to the editorial department. A bold caller could walk straight in to the city desk. It seemed that a duplicate of her first visit to the Pittsburg *Dispatch* might be enacted here. So one day she dropped by "informally" to have an interview with the city editor.

But the editor was in no mood to receive job applicants. The *World* was better equipped with the magical new instruments, telephones, than any other paper in America, and the majority of them were on the city desk. The editor was busy answering them, yelling for reporters, and poring over copy. He paid little attention to Nellie, after telling her to go home and write a letter to the paper stating her qualifications.

Using her ears, however, Nell was able to pick up one interesting tidbit of news before she left. Pulitzer was sponsoring a balloon flight out in St. Louis!

"Who's going up to cover the story, do you know?" she

asked the office boy eagerly. He looked at her and shook his head.

"The boss don't talk things over with me much," he said with heavy sarcasm. "Did you think you'd go, maybe?"

Nell evaded. "You couldn't get me in to talk to him, could you?"

Her tone pleaded, but the office was hot and airless and the boy was presumably too uncomfortable to be impressed.

"Nope, I couldn't. You nor nobody else. He don't like callers. 'Specially women. I've seen you hanging 'round here before. You might just as well stop coming."

It was the answer of all men to women who wanted jobs, Nellie thought rebelliously. Office boys and editors alike always said no. She would show this gawky kid he couldn't discourage her any more than her halfbrothers once had. She would get a job here the way she had on the Pittsburg *Dispatch*, by keeping after it. If she couldn't see Mr. Pulitzer, she would write to him.

Write to him she did, that very night, offering her services as girl reporter to make the balloon ascent.

But scores of other writers had the same idea.

Nellie peered into her box at the syndicate office a dozen times a day. Eventually she found a brief note there. On the *World* letterhead was the statement that a writer had been selected to make the ascent with the balloonist. The lucky winner of course was a man.

The dynamic *World* did not sound any more open to girl reporters than did the lofty *Sun*. But the syndicate work was at an end. Nellie became worried.

Then something happened that made her desperate: she lost a purse which contained most of her savings. The New York job must come now or never. She donned the Paris gown, adjusted the veil of the little French hat, put on a thumb ring which she believed brought luck, and set forth determined to get in to see the great Joseph Pulitzer.

Indian summer heat smothered New York like a feather bed. Those whose duties did not force them abroad stayed quietly behind drawn shutters. The few sweating male pedestrians carried their coats, fanned their faces with their hats. The horse-drawn stages scarcely seemed to move, and smart carriages were scarce on Fifth Avenue. In a short time the yacht race scheduled between the *Thistle* and the *Volunteer* would bring crowds down the bay to watch the most exciting sports event of the fall season, but now the city's affluent lingered on in Newport and Bar Harbor. The city had an air of desolation. It made Nellie feel lonely and sad.

She gave her talisman ring an extra twist, turned into the *World* building, and went up the narrow stairs toward the editorial room. Messenger boys and "leg men" who brushed past her eyed her curiously. And this time as she headed for the city desk she was intercepted by the office boy.

"You here again?" he demanded. "I thought you were supposed to write a letter."

"It didn't help. Now I intend to see Mr. Pulitzer."

The boy snickered.

"That's a good one!"

"I mean it. Tell him I'm here, please."

Obviously she did mean it. The boy regarded her with pop eyes.

"Look Miss Bly— that was your name, wasn't it—*Bly*? Like in the song?"

"Yes. Nellie Bly."

"Well, Nellie Bly, even President Cleveland couldn't get in to see Mr. Pulitzer today." He extended his arms and waved her backward. "He's having a big conference with the managing editor. Nobody can see him. *Nobody.*"

"*I* shall see him."

She shoved past him. The boy did not dare seize her and he could not stop her. Over his shoulder he appealed to the city desk.

"Hey, somebody help me. It's *her* again! This time she just wants to see Mr. Pulitzer."

The copy editor didn't trouble to look up. He waved a pencil in the direction of the thin partition which separated the editorial room from Pulitzer's private office. "The boss doesn't feel good today. Even the squeak in the door bothers him. Get her out of here, somebody, and do it quick."

A rewrite man rose wearily to the task. Then he saw Nellie and his look changed. A couple of reporters were trying to lead her to the stairs, but she wasn't going. The reporters did not know what to do. Getting rid of cranks was routine in an editorial room. But this girl was different. Even if she did want to see Pulitzer, she was pretty and dressed like a fashion plate, and she talked sense. You couldn't throw her out. After a while the copy editor discovered he was alone. The entire staff was arguing not unhappily with the visitor. He joined the crowd.

"I told you to write a letter——" he began crossly.

"And I wrote it. Here's the answer." She laid it out.

"All right. You can't go up in a balloon. Now what do you want?"

"I want to write stories for the *World.*"

The editor laughed. So did the men about him. "Everybody in America wants to write for the *World.*"

"But I can do the kind of thing you'll publish."

"You think what the *World* needs is a lady writer?" he asked.

She flushed. She knew what he was thinking. Since the Civil War there had been a few "lady newspaper writers" in America—widows of colonial publishers who had tried to carry on when their husbands died, suffragettes who edited propaganda sheets, contributors of feminine features. Nellie had heard of one, variously known as Sally Joy and Penelope Penfeather, whose work costume was a white satin gown and who wrote flowery essays on love and domestic matters and brought them to the office tied with blue ribbon. Such work ranked as "filler" when patent medicine and Pears' Soap ads were scarce. It was never taken seriously.

But Nell also knew this was no time to lose her temper. She said with quiet dignity. "Will you tell Mr. Pulitzer I'm here, or shall I just walk in?"

It was a three-hour battle and the *World* staff lost. The city editor knocked at Joseph Pulitzer's door and opened it.

"The lady's name is Nellie Bly," he announced from the doorway. "She says she's a newspaper woman and a good one. Maybe she is. She don't give up easy, I'll say that."

The door closed. Nell was in the room where Joseph Pulitzer sat in conference with John Cockerill, his managing editor.

The two men were a study in contrasts. Pulitzer, still in his forties, was growing thin from a progressive illness and was losing his sight. But his head remained leonine, with thick gray-black hair and a reddish beard. His forehead was wide, his nose long and aquiline. His skin was delicate, and the pince-nez through which he peered reddened the area between his eyes. Mr. Cockerill on the other hand was dignified, well-groomed, conventional in appearance. He did not look like a person who could have taken part in a shooting. Both men obviously were displeased at the interruption, and for a moment Nell feared she would not be permitted to stay. Then Cockerill rose and reluctantly offered her a chair.

Mr. Pulitzer stared at her.

"Nellie Bly! That's not your real name, of course. Who are you, a lady writer?"

He too was mocking her. Nell felt her cheeks grow hot.

"I am Elizabeth Cochrane and I am a reporter, Mr. Pulitzer."

"What do you want?"

"I'd like to work for the *World*."

"If you're a *reporter*, you've had experience," he challenged. "What have you done, Miss Bly?"

58

Nell produced a packet of clippings.

"I've worked for the Pittsburg *Dispatch*. I covered most of the news runs, and did features besides. I investigated conditions among Pittsburg factory women and mill-workers. I checked bad tenements. I went to Mexico and wrote about peons, prisons, and corruption in government there. I might be doing that yet, but the government objected. I couldn't write well in a Mexican jail!" she added wryly.

Mr. Pulitzer became suddenly attentive. The girl was spirited and incisive in manner. Perhaps he felt the same energy, the same vital spark in her that he himself possessed. Working girls! Prisons! Investigations! Corruption in government! They spoke the same language—the language of born crusaders.

But it was his nature to be cagey and suspicious. Maybe she was bluffing. Maybe she was a spy for Dana.

"Name a subject you could write about that the *World* might be interested in," he commanded. "Give me one idea."

Nellie waited a moment. She was prepared for this. It was the opening she wanted and she had her answer ready. But she had a sense of the dramatic. She would time it properly.

"Well?" snapped Pulitzer. "Not even one, Miss Bly?"

Cockerill leaned back and smiled. Female writers! His expression said, "I told you so. Recipes. Doilies."

"I want to feign insanity," said Nellie Bly clearly. "I want to get myself committed to the asylum on Blackwell's Island

and find out how the insane poor are treated and then write the story."

Both men sat up suddenly. Pulitzer's nostrils quivered. Cockerill blew out his breath with a loud puff. This girl hit hard. Insanity was the most feared subject in the newspaper world and its discussion taboo. As for Blackwell's Island, the toughest male reporter could be excused for refusing an assignment there. It was a place of horror. For a young girl to offer to go there, voluntarily—alone. . . .

It was impossible, of course. Yet what a story! *What a story.* . . .

Half an hour later Nellie left the *World* office with twenty-five dollars in her pocket, an advance on the idea she had left for the great Joseph Pulitzer to ponder over. But she knew as she closed his office door, as certainly as she knew when he called her back three days later, that she had taken the *World* by surprise attack.

CHAPTER VI

FANTASTIC ASSIGNMENT

IT WAS Managing Editor Cockerill who received Nellie when she was ushered in by an admiring and much subdued office boy.

"Mr. Pulitzer asked me to check this plan of yours to feign insanity," he told her sharply. "If you undertake it, you *must* go through. If you fail, you will make a laughing-stock of yourself and of the *World*. You really believe you can do it in a way that will fool the public, the police, and the doctors?"

"I am sure I can," said Nellie confidently. It was no business of his that her knees were shaking.

"You can endure living among the insane as one of them, as an inmate of an asylum? You have thought the matter over seriously?"

She had thought of nothing else since she had suggested the story to Mr. Pulitzer. She was not sure how insane patients behaved, but she had decided it would be to react logically to illogical beliefs. If you imagined yourself in great danger, sitting in a corner shaking with terror, trying to run away, even screaming with fear would be natural enough to you, and only insane to those who knew you had nothing to be afraid of. If you imagined yourself Cleopatra or Little Eva or Napoleon, you would behave as they would. It would seem sensible to you, but it would make you appear completely mad to observers. However, Nellie knew she could not take chances simulating a mild form of lunacy. She would need to do something spectacular. So she had been spending her time reading mysteries, horror tales, ghost stories, filling her mind with weird fantasies. She had passed hours before her mirror, practicing grimaces. She had muffled a rehearsal of wild screams in her bed pillow. The thought of actually living in a madhouse gave her chills, but it would give her her chance. She would not back down, whatever happened.

"I'll endure what's necessary to get my story," she said quietly. "When do I begin?"

"As soon as you feel prepared." Cockerill looked at her solemnly. "This is to be a true and accurate story, remember. The inner workings of asylums for the insane are kept hidden from the press and the public by white-capped nurses, bolts, and bars. We want to learn them, whatever they are. We do not ask you to go there for the sake of making sensational revelations. Give praise or blame as you feel it is due and tell the truth as you see it. If the inmates are treated well, say so. If they are not, put every detail of their wrongs into your story."

"Who am I supposed to be?" asked Nellie.

They finally decided Nell should become Nellie Brown.

It was a common name. The initials would correspond with those on her linen. The paper would be able to follow the record of her movements under it.

"But see to it no one suspects you are working for the *World*," Cockerill cautioned. "If some reporter on another paper guesses——"

"No one will," Nellie assured him.

It had been agreed she would take steps which would lead to her incarceration strictly on her own. Everything seemed settled now but one last question. No one had volunteered the answer. She had to ask it.

"After I get into the asylum," she demanded, "how will you get me out?"

"I don't know," admitted Cockerill bluntly. "But we will manage it."

She took a deep breath.

"When?"

"That is impossible to say. Reasonably soon, I hope."

Reasonably soon! It could mean a long time, in that grim building on Blackwell's Island.

Well, the sooner she started, the sooner she would be out with her story. She shook Mr. Cockerill's hand and went home to make her final preparations.

She laid out the clothing she was to wear, making sure there were no identification marks but the N.B. initials. She took a warm bath, gave her hair a good brushing, for she was not certain when she would be able to give attention to her toilette again. She went to bed early but could not sleep and got up and practiced her role, peering into

63

the mirror by flickering gaslight. She made a last entry in her diary. "I am in a fit mood for my mission and come what may I am determined not to shirk." She put her head firmly on the pillow again. But it was almost daylight before the *World's* girl reporter fell into troubled dozing.

The next morning, Monday, she put on a gray flannel dress, a small hat trimmed in brown with a veil, and brown shoes. She took a handbag with a few belongings, including a black memorandum book in which she had scribbled. Her little room had never appeared so attractive to her as at the last glance before she closed the door on it. So much could happen to her before she saw it again!

She felt she could not eat breakfast, for her nervousness gave her the symptoms of seasickness. But she drank some coffee and told her landlady she might be away for a few days.

In a city directory she selected at random a cheap lodginghouse, called The Temporary Home for Females, at 84 Second Avenue. She arrived there before noon. As she walked across a little paved yard to the entrance, the place reminded her of the dingy houses in Pittsburg where she had learned so much about the unhappy lot of the working girl. It had the same peeling paint, cracked windowpanes, unswept vestibule. She would seem to be a suitable inmate of such a place. She had no money with her but seventy-three cents, wrapped in a piece of thin white paper. When a penniless girl here appeared to lose her mind, there would be but one place she could be taken—the insane ward for the poor, on Blackwell's Island in the East River.

Nell stood for a second, her hand on the bell. There was still time. She could go back. Then she pulled the handle. The resulting peal sounded to her loud enough for a church chime. She assumed a look maidens wore in pictures called "Dreamy" and "Far Away" and waited.

In a few moments the door was flung open by a young girl with uncombed yellow hair and a dirty face.

"Whatcha want?" she demanded.

"Is the matron in?" Nell asked in a faint voice. She reached for the doorpost to steady herself. But the girl was not paying her any attention.

"Go in the back parlor. She'll come by and by," she said indifferently and went off down the hall.

Nell found the back parlor a dismal box of a room. She sat in a sagging chair and waited for what seemed a very long time. Finally a harassed-looking woman came in.

"I am Mrs. Stanard," she said. "What do you want?"

"I want a room here for a few days, if you can accommodate me," said Nell.

"Where do you come from?" Mrs. Stanard questioned.

"I have just arrived from Cuba." Nell had decided to put to use her recently acquired Spanish. It gave a foreign touch, and Cuba was too far away to check on.

"Where's your gripsack?" The woman's eyes were suspicious.

"It is with my trunks. They will be delivered to me as soon as I have an address."

"Where do you live in Cuba?"

Nell had her answer ready.

"An estate near Havana," she said and added a few phrases in Spanish.

The woman obviously did not understand her, but she appeared impressed. Nell could almost hear her mind working. She was thinking that here was a newcomer to New York, foreign, respectable-looking, maybe even rich, if she had trunks. Perhaps a good permanent boarder.

"We are crowded here. I haven't got a single room for you right now. But a girl is leaving later in the week. Until then you can double with one of the others."

Nell nodded. "What will it cost?" she asked.

"We charge thirty cents a night."

Nell nodded again. "I want to go to the room now," she said. "I feel tired." She counted out thirty cents and headed for the stairs.

The day and the night that followed were long remembered in The Temporary Home for Females.

At noon the lodgers learned a Cuban girl had joined them. She felt ill and was sleeping off a headache but would be down in time for supper. She showed up then, a pretty little thing, they said, when the newspapers came later to interview them. But she had a scared look in her eyes. She sat down at the table and took part in the conversation at first. But she hadn't finished her fried potatoes before she began to shake and look queer. Suddenly she jumped up and ran to the sitting room and when they followed her she was huddled in a corner, crying and shivering.

A couple of the lodgers tried to quiet her but couldn't. Finally Matron Stanard came in and took charge.

66

"What are you crying about? Are you in some kind of trouble?" she demanded.

Nell did not answer. She only cried harder. When she did speak it was in Spanish. One of the roomers had taken Spanish lessons and tried to talk to her. But Nell's only answer was, "My mind—it goes blank. My mind goes blank."

"What's your name? Tell us that. You can remember that much can't you?" demanded the matron.

Nell hesitated. What was the Spanish equivalent for Brown. Marina? Or was it Moreno? She mumbled something like it.

"You told me your name was Brown when you came this morning."

"I guess I did."

"Why, if it's something else?"

Nell looked helpless. "I'm lost," she whispered. "I can't remember. . . ."

"Where do you live?"

"In the hacienda," Nell told her. "What am I doing here? I want the peons to wait on me. Call them, please."

"*Peons*? What are they?"

The lodgers clustered around, kind, curious, and a little afraid.

"She thinks she's somebody important," said one. "Got an estate in Spain or somewhere and all that. I think she's loony."

"Maybe she is, at that. People can go off all of a sudden, they say."

"The poor thing. . . ."

But Matron Stanard would not have boarders go crazy in her house. "She just had a long trip and she's worn out," she said firmly. "I'll put her to bed and she'll be all right in the morning. Come with me, Miss Brown."

Nell went obediently, as far as the door. Then she began to fight, struggling and clawing when they tried to lead her away.

"I want my hat and gloves," she shrieked. "Get me my things. I want to go home."

To quiet her they were finally brought and she put them on. She sat in a chair in a corner then for a long time in brooding silence, while the others moved cautiously about her. When bedtime came Mrs. Stanard approached her again.

"Time to go to your room——"

"Go to bed *here,* with all these crazy women in the house?" Nell screamed. "I've got to protect myself. Get me a pistol. I want my pistol."

"You haven't got a pistol," protested the now distracted Mrs. Stanard. Then at the look in Nell's eyes she backed away.

"You've stolen it, then. I always have a pistol. How can I shoot people who come after me, if I don't have a pistol?"

Hours passed. No one slept. The alarmed lodgers took turns watching Nell.

"Poor girl, she's loony for fair!"

"So young, too. It's awful, her mind going like that. But it ain't safe havin' her around. . . ."

"I told the matron that. I pay thirty cents a night for my bed and I got to get some sleep in it."

"If they don't get her out soon, I'm movin'. I wouldn't stay around here with one like that for all the Vanderbilt money. . . ."

Nell began raving again.

At dawn Mrs. Stanard called the police. She put on her own coat and hat, tied Nell's veil, and went with her as she was taken through the gray deserted streets to the Essex Market Police Station.

Nell played her part well. It was hard to be dragged along pavements and down dirty unswept hallways. But she continued to scream about her lost pistol and fight to get free.

At the station two policemen held her before the desk of a judge whose name was Duffy. He was an amiable little Irishman and he heard the story and looked at her sympathetically. Then he said in a kind tone, "Come forward and lift your veil, Miss."

"I will not lift my veil," Nell replied haughtily.

"It is a rule of the court. If you were the Queen of England you would have to raise your veil here."

"I am not the Queen. And I shall not raise it."

The judge did not press the matter. He turned to Mrs. Stanard again.

"You say you know nothing about her, not even her real name. Did you look for labels in her clothes? Or papers in her bag?"

Mrs. Stanard sniffed. "In her bag's nothing but a note-book and forty-three cents wrapped up in a bit of paper, and a handkerchief with the initials N.B., which could be Nell Brown the way she said, I suppose. She's got on a chemise, too, marked N.B. We couldn't find anything else."

The judge looked at Nell's hands. "Maybe she's an adventuress," he said. "But she looks like a lady. She reminds me of my sister. Well, maybe the newspapers can turn up some relatives."

Nell's heart did a flipflop, and with reason. She knew what would happen when the newspaper offices got word of the mystery girl. Leg men would come in droves. They would ask her questions—hundreds of questions. . . .

But playing crazy was not so hard now. She had been awake all night and under a severe strain. Her eyes were heavy and bloodshot, her face pale, her body drooped with fatigue. Under a barrage of inquiries from the newsmen, she felt and looked hunted.

"Publish her story. Try to find out who she is," the judge finally urged reporters. "I've telegraphed for an ambulance to take her to Bellevue. The doctors there will know how sick she is."

Nell gripped the side of the hard chair in which the police had placed her and where they now held her. Police, judge, reporters. And now doctors. . . .

When the ambulance surgeon arrived, he and the judge spoke in undertones, but Nell could catch words.

". . . the girl seems to have lost her memory. . . ." It was the Judge speaking.

". . . she's pretty and refined-looking," came from the doctor.

"I feel sorry for the child . . . be kind to her . . . perhaps the newspapers . . ."

"I dislike to take her in the ambulance."

"If you don't I shall have to send her in a coach. . . ."

Finally the surgeon came over to Nellie. "Put out your tongue," he told her.

"I don't want to," she said. "That's for sick people. I'm not sick. I just want my pistol."

But the doctor looked at her tongue and took her pulse and listened to her heartbeats. He didn't need an instrument for that, Nell thought; her heart was pounding wildly. He seemed to attach some great significance to the fact. He brought out a light and examined the pupils of her eyes. Nell managed to stare unblinkingly into the light and this too impressed her examiner. He looked at her accusingly.

"What drugs have you been using?" he asked her.

Drugs? What did he mean?

"I don't know what *drugs* are," she answered truthfully.

"The pupils of her eyes have looked like that ever since she came to the house, big and black. They haven't changed once," put in Matron Stanard.

What a lie, Nell thought. Mrs. Stanard had not looked at her eyes.

"Belladonna," the doctor suggested.

Nell protested again.

"All that's wrong with my eyes is I'm a little nearsighted. You have no right to keep me here like this. Find my trunks. I want to go home."

The doctor was making notes.

"Where is home?" he asked.

"Cuba. At least, I *think* it's Cuba. . . ." She sounded frightened and confused.

"All right," said the doctor. "I'll take you home. Come along with me."

Nell closed her eyes so no one would see the gleam of triumph in them. She knew the doctor was agreeing only to get her to go with him peaceably in the big ambulance wagon; that he would make no move to take her home but would carry her off to Bellevue. He clearly thought she was crazy, as did the judge and the policemen, and the reporters and the women at the Home for Females. She had succeeded in the first part of her undertaking. But the doctors at the hospital, the specialists. Could she fool them?

She must. She was so tired her head reeled. Her courage was at its lowest. But her ordeal was only for a few days. There were women put away, helpless women, sent to these places to spend their lives. She had to find out about them, the way they were treated, the way they lived, and tell their history. She was a crusading reporter for a crusading newspaper. She'd bring back her story.

She got up, swaying a little, and caught at the ambulance doctor's arm.

72

"I'll go with you," she said with dignity. "Take me to the dock where I catch the boat for Cuba."

"She'll get a boat all right. But not for Cuba," she heard the policeman who had brought her in say as he walked away. "Her trip'll be to Blackwell's Island."

CHAPTER VII

BELLEVUE

NELL was bundled unceremoniously into the ambulance wagon. She thought gratefully of the judge's kindly face and his words in her behalf. But she suspected they would do little good. As the wagon banged and bumped over the cobblestones she felt as though she were in a tumbrel on the way to the guillotine. The doctor did not speak to her until they arrived at Bellevue. And little time was wasted on her in the receiving room there. A few questions, and an order was issued to take her directly to the insane pavilion.

"Who takes her?" the ambulance surgeon demanded.

"You do. You brought her in."

With her "escort" Nellie started down a long bleak corridor. But her steps slowed, faltered. From the men's ward came the sound of shouts and groans and curses. Somewhere she heard a woman scream. Suddenly the ordeal ahead of her seemed too much. Exhausted from lack of sleep and lack of food, for one second she would have turned back.

But she still had sense of humor enough to appreciate the doctor's crude effort at kindness.

74

"Those carpenters are certainly making a racket," he said reassuringly. "They're doing some repair work in there. Don't let their noise scare you."

He really must think her hopeless to expect her to believe that, she thought.

The path ahead of her, the dreary, uncarpeted hall, shortened. She saw large iron doors opening off of it, fastened by padlocks. The doctor took her through one into the women's ward.

It was a bare gray room furnished only with iron cots, lockers, and straight, uncomfortable chairs. The young Irish girl sweeping the floor gazed at Nell with sympathy as she walked in. Nell wanted to smile at her but she held her blank stare and simply passed by. A nurse came up, spoke with the doctor, and then turned to Nell.

"Take off your hat," she ordered.

"I am waiting for the boat," said Nell with all the dignity she could muster. "I must keep my hat on."

The doctor made a sign but the nurse ignored it.

"She might as well find it out now as later," she said. She pulled out Nell's hatpins and removed the hat by force. "You're not going on any boat," she said over Nell's protests. "You're in the Bellevue insane pavilion."

Even though it had been her goal, the words gave Nell a shock. How much more terrible they would have been if she had been the hapless victim she seemed.

Already her mind was hard at work formulating the first paragraphs of her story. From the very beginning mental patients met with indifference, incompetence, and even deliberate cruelty. It was wrong and the world should know about it.

The doctor and nurse left and Nell looked about her. She made the fourth patient in the ward. The other three were sitting dejectedly on their cots. Nell spoke to them, but only one, a middle-aged woman with a tired, worried face, answered her.

Her name was Anne Neville, she said, and she had been a working woman, a chambermaid, until her health had given way. Her nephew who was a waiter had sent her to a Sisters' Hospital to be treated. But he had lost his job and had been unable to pay her expenses there. So he had had her transferred to Bellevue.

"But why are you in this ward? If you just had a physical breakdown, you don't belong here," said Nell.

Miss Neville did not know. "The doctors keep asking me so many curious questions," she said. "Sometimes it seems as if they are trying to confuse me. When I say I gave out from overwork, they don't listen to me. And it's useless to say anything to the nurses."

Nellie was aghast. The woman seemed as sane as she was. After a bit she tried to talk to the girl on the next cot. Her remarks were very silly. However, Nell reminded herself, she had met girls just as foolish in the Pittsburg boardinghouses.

The third woman, whose name Miss Neville said was Mrs. Fox, would not even try to talk with Nell. She only shook her head and whispered over and over, "I'll never get well. It's hopeless, hopeless . . . !"

Nell collapsed on her cot and tried to rest. But, exhausted as she was, sleep would not come. The events of the night had been too disturbing. And this was only the beginning.

In the afternoon a boy entered the ward leading his mother, an old German woman named Mrs. Shanz. She did not look at all insane to Nell, only lost, as poor old people often did. As soon as her son left, she asked for something to work on. The nurse brought her some mending. She did it quickly and well.

It was almost dark when a doctor in charge of the ward appeared on his rounds. He eyed Nell curiously.

"I've seen that face before," she heard him say to the head nurse, Mrs. Scott, who accompanied him. Nell knew she must act before he came up with any suspicions. She ran toward him with a great show of eagerness.

"You know me? Tell them who I am. Make them send me home."

"Where did you come from?" he asked her.

"You know. From Cuba."

He looked around the ward and then drew Nell to one side. "You can tell the truth to me," he said in a low voice. "Are you a woman of the town?"

His tone was more insulting than his words. But she tried to ignore his insinuation.

"Of what town? Havana is far away from here."

"You know what I mean. Are you a *street* woman?"

Nell was so angry she almost forgot herself. Finally she choked out, "I do not know what that is."

"Do you let men provide for you?"

She longed to slap his face. Instead she said, "Of course. My father always provided for me. He would pay you well."

He had little more to say to her after that, but she heard him tell Nurse Scott, "Positively demented. She needs to be put where she will be taken care of."

Nell realized she had been passed upon by a second medical expert. Her regard for the ability of the doctors in charge of these cases shrank to almost nothing. From such superficial tests how could even an expert tell whether a patient was sane or not? Yet it appeared they had the authority to make diagnosis. When a little later a reporter appeared and asked to interview Miss Nellie Brown, Nell threw a blanket over her head to conceal her features. But she need not have troubled. The nurse would not let the reporter come near her. In amazement Nell heard her tell him her case was hopeless.

She was to have one more visitor before the day was through. Dr. Braisted was a handsome man, kind, sympathetic, and so charming that Nell found it more than difficult to keep up her role. She would have much preferred he did not believe her insane. But their talk was brief.

"Where did you live in Cuba?" he asked her. Nell rambled on about her plantation. Finally she demanded, "Don't you remember me? I remember you." He shook his head and departed.

The ward grew dark now and a nurse lighted a gas jet. Another patient was brought in, a girl no more than twenty-five years old, registered as Tillie Mayard. She was burning with fever. She told Nell she had been taken from a sickbed and brought here by friends for treatment for nervous debility. Obviously she had no idea this was the insane pavilion and Nell did not have the heart to tell her.

At six-fifteen the nurse in charge announced she wanted to leave and ordered them all to bed. She took every bit of Nell's clothing from her, made it into a bundle labeled "Brown," and carried it away. Then she gave her the same kind of garment worn by the others, a short cotton-flannel gown barely reaching her knees, thin and ragged from endless washings. Looking at the women about her, with their tortured faces and wispy hair, in their absurd garments, Nell felt it would be hard to go lower in loss of human dignity. She crawled into her hard bed, wrapped the thin blanket about her, and laid her head on a pillow stuffed with straw.

Above her was a barred window. Presently she heard the click of the iron door. She was alone and defenseless, locked in with the insane.

Yet what she felt was not fear but pity, a great compassion for these poor suffering victims. She did wonder dismally what would happen to them all in case of fire. The creaky old room was a firetrap, and they were sealed inside of it.

But if fire came she would know it, for there was little sleep that night. The sick girl tossed and moaned. The night nurses clumped up and down the corridor outside, their boot heels resounding. The ambulance gong sounded under the windows. The male patients howled. And when dawn broke the attendants began beating noisily for their own breakfasts, the eggs denied the patients. It was not a period of much repose.

Nor was there much for several days except a routine of physical discomfort, mental misery, and endless questions. But at six o'clock the following Sunday morning a nurse yanked the covers from Nell's bed and tossed her bundle of clothes back to her.

"Get washed and dressed," she commanded. "This is your big day."

She examined Nell's fingernails and then clipped them short. Nell got the significance of the act. If the doctors agreed as to her lack of sanity and if reporters from rival newspapers did not unmask her, before night she would be on her way to the unknown horrors of the madhouse.

She looked at her ward companions and the pathos and tragedy and horror of it all convulsed her. Perhaps her own mind wasn't too sound, to have sought such an experience as this.

The Bellevue staff which would decide her fate was assembled. The members sat about a table. Three had already seen her separately, Dr. Field, Dr. Braisted, and Dr. Fitch. Also in the room were the warden, whose name was O'Rourke, and Nurse Scott. But before the doctors began their final examination of her, the reporters had one more chance to question Nell, and their questions were sharp. The man from the *Sun* in particular gave her trouble and when he looked straight at her and blurted out, "I know you're not Nellie Brown," she almost stopped breathing.

"Who am I then?" she asked, trying to look sly.

"Our office is flooded with love letters from fellows who say you've run off and deserted them. But I think you're Lottie Peters, the long-lost sweetheart of Emile Voitier of New Orleans. *Are you Lottie?*" he demanded, coming close and staring directly into her eyes.

"Is Lottie from Cuba?" she asked. She assumed a pose of deep melancholy. "*I'm* not anybody's sweetheart." But she knew she had to get rid of the reporters and quickly. She turned to the nurse and suddenly began screaming. "Make them go away. Make them get out!" She stared at them wildly.

"You've done it now. Better leave before Dr. Field catches you," the nurse warned the newsmen. "She can't tell you a thing anyhow. Her memory's gone."

The reporters retreated. Dr. Field led Nellie away. And on the afternoon of that unforgettable Sunday, September 25, 1887, Nellie Brown Marina Moreno, having been duly examined by four eminent physicians from Bellevue Hospital, and having been found to be suffering from "dementia with delusions of persecution," and having been "duly committed by order of the Supreme Court," though knowing herself to be completely sane, was handed a moth-eaten shawl and half led, half dragged with the other "condemned" back to the ambulance wagon which was to take her on the last lap of her trip to Blackwell's Island Madhouse.

As the wagon bumped toward the East River Wharf, Nell relaxed a little. But for a moment only. There were new horrors.

The ambulance attendant's breath smelled of whisky. He looked at Nell with an insinuating grin and put an arm about her, drawing her to him. Loathing gave her strength and she flung him off.

When the patients were transferred to the Blackwell's Island barge, she found it filthy. The air in the cabin was foul. The matrons, coarse and massive women, chewed tobacco and glared in a terrifying way. Nell feared them more than her fellow passengers, among whom were Anne Neville, looking bewildered, the sick girl, Tillie Mayard, and the old German mother, Mrs. Schanz. There also were half a dozen who were clearly unbalanced, and a woman with an enormous bonnet and dirty basket filled with scraps who appeared wildly demented. Not in her most hideous nightmare had Nell ever envisioned such a company.

It was four o'clock when the boat docked and the patients were herded ashore. Horror helped Nell play her role.

"This isn't Cuba. What is this place?" she demanded frantically of a matron.

The woman grinned at her and spat out the words with a sort of vicious satisfaction. "It's Blackwell's Island, where they keep insane people like you," she said. "You'll never get out of here, dearie. *Never.*"

CHAPTER VIII

THE PAPERS SAY

FOUR DAYS after Nellie Bly left the *World* editorial room and dropped out of sight, three New York newspapers, the *Herald*, the *Evening Telegram*, and the *Sun*, brought news of her whereabouts to apprehensive Editor Cockerill. She appeared in their headlines as THE BEAUTIFUL WRECK and as THE INSANE GIRL WHO HAS NO MEMORY OF HER PAST.

The *World* of course ignored the existence of the mysterious stranger. Knowing the inside story and watchfully waiting the outcome, Pulitzer's paper diverted its readers during these anxious days with such topics as *William Rockefeller and His New Mansion Up the Hudson*, and *That Wonderful Cipher—The Revelation Disclosed by Shakespeare's Tombstone*, which some authorities thought proved that Sir Francis Bacon wrote Shakespeare's plays. The *Sun*, published by Charles Dana, Pulitzer's fiercest antagonist, went for Nell's sad plight the whole way, much to the secret gloating of both Pulitzer and Cockerill.

WHO IS THIS INSANE GIRL? asked the *Sun*, in a two-column front-page story on September 25. "She is pretty, well-dressed, and speaks Spanish. She wandered into Matron Stanard's Home for Females—Asked for a pistol to protect herself—Is her name Marina?"

THE NELLIE BROWN MYSTERY.

Her Story as Told from Day to Day by the City Newspapers.

[From the Sun, Sunday, Sept. 28.]

WHO IS THIS INSANE GIRL?

SHE IS PRETTY, WELL DRESSED AND SPEAKS SPANISH.

She Wandered Into Matron Stenard's Home for Women and Asked for a Pistol to Protect Herself—Is Her Name Marina?

A modest, comely, well-dressed girl of nineteen, who gave her name as Nellie Brown, was committed by Justice Duffy at Essex Market yesterday for examination as to her sanity. The circumstances surrounding her were such as to indicate that possibly she might be the heroine of an interesting story. She was taken to the court by Matron Irene Stenard, of the Temporary Home for Females, at 84 Second avenue. The matron said that Nellie came to the Home alone about noon on Friday, and said she was looking for her trunks. She was dressed in a gray flannel dress trimmed with brown, brown silk gloves, a black straw sailor's hat trimmed with brown, and wore a thin gray illusion veil. The closest questioning failed to elicit any satisfactory account of her. During the night she frightened the minister by insisting that she should have a pistol to protect herself. She said that she had had money in a pocketbook, but somebody took it away from her. Her voice was low and mild and her manner refined. Her dress was neat-fitting. The sleeves were of the latest style.

The girl had in her pocket thirty-three cents wrapped in white tissue paper, and a black memorandum book, in which there were some rambling and incoherent writings. One sentence was: "Jay Gould sen..e people to Siberia." Justice Duffy took

Had Nellie Bly been in a position to read the New York papers at this time, she would have viewed with astonishment this whimsy of fortune. For she, who had never stood the slightest chance of getting a job on the man-staffed sheet the *Sun,* was now featured there as a figure of appealing mystery. She would certainly have read on, as Editor Cockerill did. "A modest, comely, well-dressed girl of nineteen who gave her name as Nellie Brown was committed by Justice Duffy, Essex Market, yesterday for examination as to her sanity.

"The circumstances surrounding her were such as to indicate that she might be the heroine of an interesting story," the article stated. It recounted again her arrival at Mrs. Stanard's Home. It described her fashionable dress, her voice and manner:

"In court Nellie was not even terrified into giving an account of herself when informed she was charged with insanity. The burden of her talk in reply to many questions put to her by Justice Duffy was, 'I have no father. He is dead. So is my mother. I don't know where I came from. I want my trunks. I used to live in Cuba. I want those men to go away. I don't want anything to do with reporters. Oh, how many questions they ask me!'

"The girl had in her pocket forty-three cents wrapped in white tissue paper and a black memorandum book in which there were some rambling writings. One sentence was, 'Jay Gould sends people to Siberia.'

"Justice Duffy took a good deal of interest in the girl and

telegraphed for an ambulance. A physician from Bellevue Hospital who came with it examined the girl and expressed the opinion she was demented. She was taken to the Hospital for examination as to her sanity. If pronounced insane, she will be committed permanently to the insane asylum. The doctors at Bellevue say it is the most peculiar case that has ever come into the hospital."

The following day the *Sun* continued Nell's story.

"Her memory still gone . . . no one claims the pretty, crazy girl at Bellevue. . . . Justice Duffy believes there is romance in her story, but Warden O'Rourke doubts it. . . . She has lucid moments, according to Dr. Braisted, the physician at the Insane Pavilion, when she talks sensibly enough about what is going on around her, but appears to remember nothing of her past. She is suffering from hysterical mania with delusions of persecution."

There was one more item in the *Sun* of particular interest to Editor Cockerill. This was an announcement that Nellie Brown had been pronounced "hopelessly insane" by the medical experts at Bellevue and, after due process of law, had been sent to Blackwell's Island Lunatic Asylum on Sunday, September 25.

The managing editor of the *World* looked up from the *Sun* and eyed a calendar. He marked off on it a date. If all went as it should, what a "beat" the *World* would have on its rivals! But Cockerill was an old newspaper man and did not count on beats until he had made them. The girl had started out well. She had managed to get to Blackwell's as planned. But this was a grisly business she was up to, and she was only a woman. In Cockerill's mind there remained an "if" between the *World* and its triumph. A big "if."

CHAPTER IX

MADHOUSE—THE BEGINNING

WHY had she come here? Nellie asked herself. To get a big story that would win her a place on the *World?* To write a sensational article? To help the insane poor? It was something of all of them, she decided, and the one thing more she was coming to recognize in herself, a compulsion to get into the dark places of the world and ferret out the truth.

But this time had she let it carry her too far? As she had her first look at Blackwell's Island, the dreary isolation of the place appalled her. Suppose the *World* failed to come to her rescue soon? *Suppose they never came . . . ?*

They would, of course, she told herself sternly.

The matron grasped her arm and forced her into the ambulance wagon with the rest. As they drove past the kitchen of the asylum, there was a stench so overpowering Nell held her breath. Finally the wagon stopped. She entered a gray stone building and found herself in a barren reception room filled with women. They were laughing, crying, gibbering, yet to her surprise several patients moved over and made room for Nell on a bench.

"My husband put me here," said one of them. "Who sent you?"

"The doctors," Nell told her. Her companion looked surprised. She studied Nell intently. "If you are insane, it doesn't show in your face, my dear," she said finally.

A nurse was checking in the new arrivals. Nell saw Tillie Mayard go to her and heard her pleading. She was telling about her physical illness and the fever and nervous debility it had caused. She was not insane, Miss Mayard declared, only sick. She asked to be treated with justice, to be given an opportunity to explain her case.

She spoke rationally. But the nurse paid no attention to her, simply pushed her aside. And when Mrs. Schanz came up timidly and spoke in German, the nurse, though obviously German herself, pretended not to understand her. Nell decided the girl was trying to have a flirtation with the doctor and was ashamed of her nationality. She was a good-looking, stupid blonde and her mind clearly was not on her patients.

Finally it was Nellie's turn. The nurse called out, "Nellie Brown, Dr. Kinier wants to see you."

Dr. Kinier now. Names, names, names, Nellie thought. Doctor after doctor, enough to confuse even a reporter whose job it was to remember people. And questions again. Silly questions.

"What is your name? . . . Where do you live? . . . What is the color of your eyes?"

The nurse answered that one for her. "Gray," she said, though a look would have showed they were hazel. She shoved Nell onto the scales and went through the motions of recording her weight. It was 112 pounds. But Nell had to record the reading, since the nurse had eyes only for the doctor. He appeared to be a kindly man and Nell made her usual appeal.

"I am not sick. I do not want to stay here. Please send me home."

She was familiar with procedure now. She knew he would either ignore her or try to distract her. He chose the latter.

"Do you play the piano?" he asked.

"I've played ever since I was a child."

He led her to an old-fashioned square instrument, the nurse following. Nell let her fingers run over the keys. It was hopelessly out of tune. She made a face at the discords. "How horrible!" she said.

The doctor's face agreed but the nurse put in spitefully, "We'll have to get one made to order for you."

But it wasn't herself Nell was thinking about. It was the patients. Music might help them. Perhaps she could bring a little comfort to the pathetic group. She began with a chord and as gentle melodies filled the room the talking ceased. Quietly and attentively the lonely, the old, the sick, the demented listened as Nellie Bly played to them, "Home, Sweet Home."

The supper gong stopped her. The inmates had to form in line two by two in the hall and wait to go in to the dining room. The hall was long and drafty and the weather had turned suddenly chill. They all stood shivering. Nell was surrounded by the truly insane now; many appeared completely demented. They chattered nonsense, talked to invisible people, laughed and cried for no reason. One sprightly old lady nudged Nell and winked sagely.

"Don't mind them," she advised her. "All but you and me are crazy here."

"And maybe I am," Nell thought. How long could she stand this and stay sane? Lunatics to eat with, sleep with, be considered one with. Would her mind snap under it? She wasn't here for self-pity, however, but to learn of the trials of others. She put her thoughts on that.

Finally the doors were opened and the waiting women marched into the narrow dining room. At each place Nell saw a bowl of something which probably passed as stew. Next to it was a slice of stale bread and a saucer with five wilted prunes. The patients immediately went into action. A fat woman began to grab up the bread and prunes from the places near her. A girl across the table snatched Nell's piece of bread, but another patient politely offered her her portion. Nell declined it with thanks. How true to their natural selves insane people seemed to remain, she thought. The selfish grew more selfish, the unselfish more generous.

She turned to look for the nurses. They sat at a table of their own, set with a fresh cloth and china dishes. On their plates were good cuts of meat, white bread, fresh fruit. Nell had eaten almost nothing for days and she eyed it hungrily.

"Could I have a piece of bread?" she called to a nurse. "I have none."

The nurse took a moldy hunk from another inmate's place and flung it down beside Nell's plate. While Nell hesitated about spreading it with the rancid butter, a spider crawled out of it. She pushed her plate away, all appetite gone. Anne Neville, who sat near her, said, "Try to force something down, dear. To have a good brain, the stomach must be cared for."

The management clearly did not share Miss Neville's point of view. Nell, sitting on the backless bench, could not choke down a mouthful.

After supper the patients flocked to the piano again and begged her to play something more. She tried simple folk songs and found Miss Mayard knew them. The girl was still ill and feverish, but she sang them beautifully.

The interlude of peace did not last long. A nurse shouted, "Bath time," and a group of the new patients were herded into a bare unheated room for tubbings. The inmates did the work at these ceremonies and Nell found herself assigned to one of the most disturbed patients in the ward. The woman, holding a great dirty rag in her hand, stood chuckling to herself beside an iron tub while a nurse stripped Nell of her clothes. Then she shoved her into the bath, which was cold. The woman began to scrub her, performing what was practically a sanding operation of Nell's delicate face and neck, soaking her long hair. She finished by throwing three buckets of icy water over her. Nell was then tossed a thin flannel slip with "Lunatic Asylum. B.I.H. 6" stamped in black on it.

As she stood shaking with cold and shock, she saw that Miss Mayard, her cheeks brilliant with fever, was being given the same treatment. Nell could not restrain herself. She turned to the nurse.

"Miss Mayard is sick. She is running a temperature. At least give her a warm nightgown."

"We don't have nightgowns here. This is *charity*," the nurse said angrily.

"But the city pays to keep places like this up. And it pays salaries to nurses to care for the patients and be kind to them."

"Well, you don't need to expect any kindness here, for you won't get it. Not in a lunatic asylum."

No, there was no kindness. One after another the helpless victims were plunged into the icy tub, the water in which was never changed. Sobbing and chilled, they were given their skimpy slips and sent dripping back to Ward 6. There a nurse went from one patient to another, using the same comb on all. Nell felt she could not bear it.

"Stop it," she begged. "Some of these women's heads are infested. I saw lice in their hair."

The nurse looked at her sneeringly.

"Don't put on airs, Miss Nellie Brown. We know all about you. There's a big story in the *Sun* that your brain cracked because you were discarded by your Latin lover. So don't think you're any better than the rest of them."

So that was what the papers said. But Nell didn't have time to consider it now.

"I'm not asking just for myself. It's for all of them——"

"You're going to be a troublemaker, I can see it." The

nurse turned to an assistant coming into the ward with a lantern. "Put Nellie Brown into a room alone tonight," she ordered. "That'll quiet her down."

The other nurse giggled.

"The noisy, saucy type, is she? Come along, Nell." She led the way down the dark hall to a cell marked 28.

The cubicle window was barred, the door bolted. Nell heard the nurse clump on down the hall, locking each cell separately. There were 1600 inmates on the Island. She had thought fire a hazard at Bellevue. But if one broke out here, not a dozen would escape.

Far into the night, her head in the puddle made by her sopping wet hair, Nell lay thinking. Why were the dangers and agonies of such an institution as this so multiplied? On an assignment at the Western Penitentiary in Pittsburg, she had been shown the progressive lock system in use there. An attendant could lock or unlock every cell on a floor with one quick motion. The method here was danger-ous and primitive. Committed without reasonable cause, overworked, poverty-stricken women lived under condi-tions too harsh for animals. Someday, if she was not wiped out by fire, pneumonia, or a berserk inmate before her deliverance came, Nellie Bly swore she would bring about reforms, many, many of them, on this Godforsaken island.

But now she was only one of them, a duly certified inmate of Ward 6, whose days were meaningless and nights endless.

The asylum day began at 5:30. Nell like all the others was outfitted with one pair of heavy, oversized boots, one pair of stockings, a sacklike calico dress, and a white straw

94

hat for "outings." In the washrooms women with running sores on their faces wiped themselves on the same towel used by all the rest. Nell avoided it by dabbing water on her eyes and drying them quickly on her skirt. As soon as their scant breakfast was eaten, the inmates were set to work making beds and scrubbing. They were required to do much of the work about the place, inside and out. They cared for the nurses' rooms and laundered their uniforms, while they themselves went neglected and unkempt. Those who could not help themselves soon became very dirty.

The work routine was broken only when the patients were taken for an airing. One day they were given a ride on the Island merry-go-round. As Nell and Miss Neville put on their comical straw hats preparatory to this excursion, Nell thought the hats looked like those worn by bathers at Coney Island. She could not help but laugh at the ridiculous getups.

But there was nothing comical in the faces in the endless line of marchers. There were vacant eyes, empty expressions, matted hair. The violent patients from the Retreat and the Lodge, where suicidal and maniacal cases were kept, were brought out too, chained together on a long cable or riding in heavy iron carts. Crippled, blind, old, young, homely, pretty, they were together, yelling, cursing, singing, praying, as the fancy took them.

Nell saw them all, noted them all, remembered them all. But it was the individual rather than the mob that brought her to tears. Miss Neville, fighting without hope; Miss Mayard, trying to rise above the outward degradation and cling to her sanity; the little old woman, almost blind, who limped in out of the cold wind and tried to remove the boots which tortured her.

A nurse ordered her to put them back on and as she started wearily across the room she bumped into the wall.

"Why can't I stay in bed?" she pleaded. "Or even have a shawl. I'm so tired and cold. God—please take me home!"

Nell had no paper and pencil with her. She could make no notes. But the stories she had to tell were written on her heart.

CHAPTER X

MADHOUSE—THE END

For five days it rained.

Nell and the other nonviolent ward patients could not go outside. They sat in the barren reception room all day long with nothing to do. It was much worse than working. Talking and moving about were forbidden. But they did whisper together sometimes.

It interested Nell that what they usually talked about was food, what they would eat when they "got back into the world." They seemed haunted by the supplies they saw in the doctors' and nurses' kitchens which they passed on the way to their "outings"—chicken, vegetables, rosy apples, raisins, fresh bread. They discussed them endlessly.

When the subject of food was exhausted, they talked of the management. Nell had learned the names of the staff now. Miss Burns, a night nurse in Ward 6, was given honorable mention for some of her kind ways. So were Dr. Ingram and one or two of the other physicians. But the patients wished the rest would act more understandingly. Nell, listening, thought it would have paid the management to hear these complaints. It appeared to her at times the attendants deliberately or ignorantly did all they could

97

to make the inmates worse. She regarded some of the rules as barbarous. Take any sane healthy woman, make her sit from 6:00 A.M. to 8:00 P.M. on a straight bench without speaking or moving, let her know nothing of the world or its doings, give her vile food and harsh treatment, and you *made* her insane, Nell concluded. She estimated two months of the treatment would drive her stark, raving mad.

Sometimes it seemed the nurses enjoyed dispatching patients to the violent ward. There was Pauline, an Irish girl with delusions of persecution, who was their special target. Pauline imagined herself in a personal battle with the devil and was in the habit of bursting out with "Three cheers! I've killed the old one. Lucifer! Lucifer!" and tearing out her hair in her agitation. One morning when a doctor was coming down the hall Nell heard a nurse whisper to the demented girl, "Here's the devil coming now. Why don't you go for him?"

Appalled that a nurse would give such instructions, Nell feared the girl would rush for him. She did not. But a little later the nurse again tried to excite her by saying a pictured minstrel on the wall was the devil. This time the suggestion worked. The girl became frantic. She began to scream and rage, "You devil, I'll give it to you." She smashed the picture and two of the nurses had to sit on her to restrain her. When they could not, she was dispatched to the violent ward.

The nurses, many of them ignorant girls themselves, found much amusement in teasing the inmates. One patient who insisted she was eighteen, though actually in her

98

twenties, went into convulsions when the nurses teased her by saying she was past thirty-five. "I'm not that old! I'm not that old!" she sobbed wildly as she was dragged away. Another, a young Hebrew woman whose husband had "put her away" because of an affair, was tormented endlessly by the nurses about her "many lovers."

When Nell spoke in defense of these patients, the nurses gave her a warning. "Watch your tongue, or we'll send *you* to the Lodge. That will cure you of interfering."

There was a time when Nell would have staged a violent scene in order to be sent there. But she knew better than to do that now. She had seen the inmates of this hellhole on their morning airings and a few who had come back to Ward 6 told of the brutal treatment: of being beaten with broom handles, choked, locked in closets, held under ice-cold water until they were senseless. They returned with cracked ribs, black eyes, broken jaws. And the ones who did these things to them were not other inmates, but the attendants. Nell was unable to regard this kind of treatment as an inevitable part of the asylum life.

She talked to one girl named Bridget McGuinness who had been sent there for throwing a stone through the nurses' kitchen window.

"The nurses at the Lodge always keep a quiet patient posted to let them know when the doctors are coming," Bridget said. "So the doctors never know what goes on. If we told, they said we made it up and we got a beating for our 'lies.' There are quiet patients who have been there for years—the nurses keep them because they do all their work. It's a heartless place. I saw a girl killed while I was there. She was very sick and the nurses threw her into a tub of ice water. The next day she was dead. The doctors never knew about the tubbing. They decided she died of convulsions."

No, Nellie Bly had no desire to get herself committed to the Lodge or the Retreat.

Sealed away from the outside world as she had been for days with no visitors, no communication from the newspaper which had sent her here, Nell lost track of time. She tried to forget her personal uneasiness in acquiring all the material she needed: evidence upon evidence of outrages that went on here, of the need for reform. Not until then would she go away and write her story, call upon the world to help these victims.

Her final discovery was the most fantastic and frightening. Although since the day she had arrived on Blackwell's Island she had ceased to feign madness and had spoken and behaved in a perfectly rational manner, no one had paid any attention to the change. She talked to the doctors whenever she could, trying to discover what chance she had of being discharged if she had to get out through her own efforts. It appeared she had almost none.

One morning she took her case directly to the head doctor, Superintendent Dent.

"What are the doctors here for?" she demanded.

"To take care of the patients and test their sanity." He spoke as if humoring a child.

"But there are sixteen doctors on the Island and I have

never seen but two of them pay any attention at all to the patients. How can a doctor judge a patient's sanity simply by saying 'Good morning' to her? It's all they do. Yet even the craziest person here knows it's useless to protest. The answer is, 'It's your imagination.' "

"You will have to believe the doctors here know their business, Miss Brown."

"Then let them examine me—give me every test. If they do, they'll find I am perfectly sane."

He smiled and patted her shoulder soothingly. "We will see."

But no tests were given her. Day after day Nell insisted. The nurses reported she was raving again.

Nell felt that only one of the doctors listened to her at all. She did not know that Dr. Ingram studied her bright eyes and alert manner, marked her intelligent conversation, and told his associates, "I have regarded her case as hopeful. She now seems to me sane." But he was overruled. Specialists had declared Nell Brown's mental illness hopeless. Her case was closed. She must spend her life on Blackwell's Island.

And time was becoming a blur to Nell. She was aware of gnawing worry, but it seemed a part of the misery in a pattern where one horrible day was indistinguishable from another.

Then one morning she heard Dr. Dent, who was writing an order, ask a nurse the date. At the reply Nell's heart almost stopped beating. To make sure she was right she counted, slowly and carefully, on her fingers. *Ten days* had passed; for *ten days* she had been a prisoner on this island. *And she had not yet had one sign of reassurance or of deliverance.*

The apprehension she had felt broke into sharp and recognized terror.

The *World* could not have forgotten her. But perhaps there had been difficulties—some legal tangle. It might even be that what she had done was against the law. After all, she was scarcely known to Mr. Pulitzer. She was not a regular member of his staff. It could be that the *World* had found itself in trouble, feared a scandal, and had simply washed its hands of her and her escapade.

The possibility had haunted her from the beginning. It was enough to drive her mad. She could become insane in reality; she felt close to it already.

And there was nothing she could do. She knew no one would believe her story, or even listen to it. Without help from the outside, she was lost.

She lay all night, sleepless, facing the consequences of her reckless action.

The following morning she took her place in the line. As she put on her "Coney Island" hat and started the dreary march with the other forlorn creatures, she felt a permanent part of the dreadful scene. Was she one of them? She had to fight to keep from crying out, from beating at the walls. She dragged one foot after the other and her eyes were as vacant and empty as her hope.

Dazed with horror, when a strange man accompanied by

a nurse came down the walk, she did not move to let them pass. But they stopped beside her.

"Nellie Brown, step out of line," the nurse ordered.

Shivering, Nell obeyed. What did this mean? What were they going to do to her now?

The man came close to her. Another doctor? An official to move her to the Retreat as punishment for her show of spirit? Was this the day Nell Brown vanished forever, and became no more than a number?

But the stranger was smiling. There was admiration in his eyes.

"I'm your lawyer," he told Nell in a whisper. "I was sent by the *World* to get you out of here."

"And none too soon," said Nellie Bly.

On the morning of Saturday, October 8, 1887, readers of the *World* took up their morning paper and saw on the front page, in the upper left hand box:

A Strange Phase of City Life

THE MYSTERIOUS GIRL WHO PUZZLED
THE DOCTORS AT BELLEVUE
SEE THE SUNDAY WORLD

By Sunday most of New York's reading public, much to the chagrin of rival newspapers, had switched to the *World*.

In it began the shocking story, BEHIND ASYLUM BARS, The Mystery of the Unknown Insane Girl.

It was a voluminous story, both ludicrous and terrible, signed with the name of a girl reporter, Nellie Bly. It challenged from the first line of its first installment. Before the series was finished, the entire country was aroused to high indignation over the treatment accorded the insane on Blackwell's Island. A veil had been ripped from the most feared and hushed-up subject on earth, insanity. An intimate report on it had been presented by a twenty-year-old girl who deliberately had had herself committed and learned the facts from personal experience.

The story showed the mistakes and oversights of many theoretical experts; it portrayed doctors and nurses who knew little of human nature. It presented a layman's observations about the insane which made sense to the public, and it suggested a whole new approach to the handling of the insane, far in advance of this year 1887.

"I always had a desire to know asylum life more thoroughly," Nellie Bly wrote, "a desire to be convinced that the most helpless of God's creatures, the insane, were cared for kindly and properly. . . . And so I determined on a plan which led me to the successful accomplishment of my mission.

"I succeeded in getting committed to the insane ward at Blackwell's Island, where I spent ten days and nights and had an experience I shall never forget. I took upon myself to enact the part of a poor unfortunate crazy girl, and felt it my duty not to shirk any of the disagreeable results that should follow. I became one of the city's insane for that length of time, experienced much and saw and heard more of the treatment accorded to this helpless class of our population, and when I had seen and heard enough, my release was secured by the *World*. I left the insane ward with pleasure and regret; pleasure that I was once more able to enjoy the free breath of heaven; regret that I could not have brought with me some of the unfortunate women who lived and suffered with me, and who, I am convinced, are just as sane as I was, and now am.

"But here let me say one thing. From the moment I entered the insane ward of the Island, I made no attempt to keep up the role of insanity. I talked and acted just as I do in ordinary life. Yet, strange to say, the more sanely I talked and acted, the crazier I was thought to be by all but one physician, whose kindness and gentle ways I shall not soon forget.

". . . The Insane Asylum on Blackwell's Island is a human rat-trap. It is easy to get in, but, once there it is impossible to get out. I had been shut off from all visitors, and so, when a lawyer came and told me I was finally leaving, I was overjoyed.

"I waved to Miss Neville and other friends I'd made who were taking a walk as I left. *Good-by—I'm going home.* But even as I said farewell on the way to freedom and life, I felt sad, for they were left behind to an existence far worse than death.

"I had looked forward so eagerly to leaving this horrible place, but when my release really came there was pain in leaving. For ten days I had been one of them. Foolishly enough, it seemed selfish to leave them to their sufferings. I felt a quixotic desire to help them by my sympathy and presence. But only for a moment. The bars were down. And liberty was much sweeter to me than ever before. Soon I was crossing the river and nearing New York. Once again I was a free girl, after ten days in the Madhouse on Blackwell's Island."

CHAPTER XI

THE TRUTH—AND NOTHING BUT THE TRUTH

STEPHEN FOSTER, the composer, had written it:

> Nelly Bly, Nelly Bly,
> Bring de broom along,
> We'll sweep de kitchen clean, my lub,
> And hab a little song.

And even as he lay dying in a charity ward at Bellevue Hospital, in 1864, he might have felt cheered to know that twenty-three years later a courageous young newspaper woman using the name from his song as a nom de plume would enter the insane ward of this same institution and make revelations which would bring about the greatest reforms in hospitals and asylums America had so far known.

Nellie Bly was indeed "sweeping de kitchen clean." Creating a character part dream, part reality, she bettered the world for others while fulfilling her own destiny. In a startling fashion she made seemingly impossible hopes come true.

The faith that George Madden and Erasmus Wilson had felt in Pittsburg's first girl reporter was more than justified now. The proud acquisition of the *World* and its vast public, Nell became known nationally almost overnight. The *World* opened up its big guns editorially in support of Nell's sensational exposure, labeling it "an act of humanity," and calling it the talk of the town and the nation. Editorials in other New York and most out-of-town papers commented on "the remarkable exploit of Nellie Bly."

"Nellie Bly's story will attract wide attention," said the Norristown, Pennsylvania, *Times*. "The investigation was not only a neat piece of journalistic enterprise, but it may lead to reforms which will be for the decided advantage of the insane."

And, from the Wheeling *Intelligencer*, came this salute: "Not so much because of the novel method she adopted to gain information she desired for the newspaper employing her, or the thrilling experiences she so courageously endured, as on account of the success of her undertaking.

"With one single exception, all examining physicians pronounced her insane, while the doctor who imagined he detected humbug had not sufficient confidence in his own judgment to protest against her confinement."

In view of Nell's disclosures, the Hamilton, Ontario, *Times* asked the obvious but shocking question, "What is to prevent doctors in collusion with interested relatives from putting sane people away?"

Paper after paper offered similar comments. "Food for thought." "There is much food for reflection in this—a young girl 'pulling the wool' over the eyes of so-called medical experts." "There is enough in this business to set people to thinking."

The New York *Sun*, stung to its circulation depths by girl reporter Nellie Bly's scoop, and seeking to minimize the importance of a mere female's findings, was forced to admit in headlines: NELLIE BLY TOO SHARP FOR ISLAND DOCTORS.

Although this paper now professed to have had doubts as to Nellie Brown's insanity from the beginning, it conceded: "Nellie Bly is intelligent, capable, and self-reliant, and, except for the matter of changing her name to Nellie Bly, has gone about the business of maintaining herself in journalism in a practical businesslike way."

In a series of interviews with doctors, nurses, and ambulance drivers who had been "taken in," the *Sun* attempted to show the other side of the coin.

"Dr. Ingram, an Island doctor, proved to be the one person she could talk to," the *Sun* reported. "She accomplished her deception with great skill, was not too talkative or inventive to give herself away." Then it added, "Dr. Ingram is a handsome man with light mustache, side whiskers, and a way with women. He was much interested in Nellie's case."

The *Sun* brought out that "the attractive Island nurses," while not regarding Nell as unruly exactly, had found her "saucy" and "inclined to run to the doctors with complaints." They had observed some things not usual about her. Unlike her lunatic companions, Nell had not even tried to grab the brass ring when she rode on the Island merry-go-round, the nurses said.

Warden O'Rourke came forward to state that he had never for a moment believed Nellie Brown to be insane, but had been overruled by public opinion and the "authorities." The ambulance driver who had tried to "bundle" with Nell on her ride to the wharves protested he had done so wholly in the interest of medical science. "If she had been really insane," he observed, "she would have thrown her arms around me. All the lunatic girls do that."

Several of the Bellevue doctors who had pronounced Nellie Brown "hopelessly insane" were mysteriously off duty when reporters came to quiz them. But young Dr. Braisted admitted he had been "bewitched and bewildered" by Nell, and that she was, at the very least, a fine actress or confidence girl. Superintendent Dent, in charge of the Island doctors, said he was greatly impressed by Nell's revelations, and would be only too glad to improve conditions in the asylum, if and when funds were forthcoming.

But, although the *Sun* did its best to save face, the honors went to the *World*. Soon after Nellie Bly's series of stories was completed, she was summoned before the Grand Jury. Before "twenty-three august men," she swore to the truth of her statements, and the jurors, headed by Assistant District Attorney Vernon Davis, asked her to accompany them on a visit to Blackwell's Island.

Supposedly the trip was shrouded in darkest secrecy, but there was no doubt news of it had leaked out.

"The trip to the Island," Nell reported in the *World,* "was vastly different from my first. This time we went on a clean new boat, while the one I had traveled on, we were told, was laid up for repairs." There were no tobacco-chewing matrons aboard this one, Nell noted.

In other respects there had been amazing changes, also. On the Island the halls were in order, the wards neat, and the kitchen spic and span. Even the patients looked cleaner than Nell had described them as being. But under examination some of the nurses made statements which contradicted each other as well as Nell's stories, and they finally admitted the Jury's contemplated visit had been known to them and to the doctors. Superintendent Dent spoke frankly about the problems in running an institution for the insane.

"I am glad you did this now, and had I known your purpose I would have aided you. We have no means of learning the way things are going except as you did," he told Nellie.

He admitted to the jurors he had no way to determine positively whether the baths Nell had been forced to take were ice cold, or what number of women were put into the same bath water. He said he knew the food was wretched and the system of locking the patients into cells deplorable, but that it was due to lack of funds. He further admitted he had no method of ascertaining whether attendants were cruel to patients, and pointed out it was hard to attract and keep good nurses on the Island because salaries there were only about seventeen dollars a month, less than was paid to servant girls, and the atmosphere was depressing. The doctors too were underpaid and it was difficult to secure the best medical men, although he declared those on the Island were competent.

When the investigation began, the nurses swore there were no such inmates as those Nellie had mentioned by name in her stories, and Nellie could not locate them. The nurses even denied a Tillie Mayard ever had been there. This was too much and Miss Mayard finally was reluctantly produced from a remote part of the Island. She had changed so much for the worse that Nellie shuddered when she saw her. Miss Anne Neville too was finally brought in, and she appeared ill and much older. But she told Nellie that since she had left the food had improved "miraculously" and so had the sanitary conditions. The nurses and doctors appeared to be more considerate, she added wonderingly. She had heard a nurse at the Retreat had been caught setting watches for the doctors' approach and had been dismissed for it.

"After all the deceptions," Nell wrote, "I hardly expected the Grand Jury would sustain me. Yet they did, and their report to the court advised all the changes I had proposed."

It was a triumphant end to her trials and tribulations in breaking in and out of the asylum. Nellie's daring idea, first designed to attract Joseph Pulitzer's attention, bore rich fruit. On the basis of her investigation, changes for the better were made not only in New York but in other American hospitals. An appropriation of three million dollars was given to Blackwell's Island for improvements.

And Nellie Bly, a member of the staff of the *World* at a high salary, was given free rein as a crusading reporter.

CHAPTER XII

LITTLE GIRL—BIG BROOM

IT WAS the fulfillment of her hope and Nellie Bly made the most of it. The experiences she had passed through had impressed her deeply, and she had learned at first hand the power of the press in righting wrongs. She promptly turned her efforts toward other reforms.

She had hardly finished her stories on Blackwell's Island when she took up the cause of the working girl once more. Because of the unregulated flood of immigrants pouring into New York City during the eighties, the plight of these young women was even worse than in Pittsburg. The daughters of poor greenhorns were hard pressed enough to go into the unprotected working marts of the city. Here, they were hired for a pittance, then fired and fed into the underworld. In rapid succession Nell wrote story after story, bringing out the tragic position of the servant girl, shopgirl, and factory girl in New York.

Posing as an inexperienced girl seeking work, in October of 1887 Nell went on a round of employment bureaus. She first visited the Germania Servant's Agency on Fourth Avenue. The knob on the door gave way as she turned it and the proprietor approached her, demanding the customary registration fee. He eyed her with insulting intimacy.

"You're a nice-looking girl and I will get you a place. Many gentlemen and ladies will pay more when the girls are as good-looking as you," he told her. After suggesting Nell live at his quarters behind the agency for "two-fifty a week with board" between jobs, he introduced her to an elderly gentleman whose wife needed an experienced "washer and ironer." In an aside Nell protested she wanted to be a chambermaid and had neither references nor experience for the job he proffered, but he proceeded to "sell" Nell to the unsuspecting gentleman as a highly competent laundress.

Nell got away on some pretext. She visited next the employment bureau of a Mrs. L. Seely on Twenty-second Street. Here again she paid her fee. She was taken to the third floor and put in a small room where women were packed as close as pickles in a barrel. At least fifty-two girls and women were in the place; groups stood on the stairs and out in the dingy hallway, waiting, endlessly waiting. But whether a girl was finally given employment or turned away because she was too tall, too short, or too heavy, because she had bangs or wore mourning, all the bureaus, Nell soon found out, exacted their fees again and again. Many girls, on the other hand, were recommended for jobs for which they were totally unsuited, as Nell had been.

"She pays her fee and is guaranteed employment," the *World* bannered Nellie Bly's servant-girl story. "She has no references; the agent knows nothing of her character; nevertheless he declares she possesses all the virtues on the calendar. Can a common thief, thus recommended, get service in New York homes?"

Yes, Nell declared, while experienced recommended girls were turned away because they did not suit the whims of some incompetent bureau head. There should be *laws* to protect both employer *and* the servant girl, this pioneer for fair labor practices insisted. Public opinion should and must curb the unscrupulous methods of New York's unrestrained employment bureaus.

It was a new idea. But the seed was planted.

Next, Nell went to work on New York's "white slaves," the girls who toiled in factories at substandard wages. Wearing a calico dress and carrying her lunch in brown wrapping paper, she started out early one morning seeking factory employment. Because of her inexperience, she was turned away from a number of plants around Bleecker and Grand streets, but finally was given a tryout in a smaller box factory on Elm Street. The work was dirty, she was told in a masterpiece of understatement, and beginners received no wages for the first two weeks. If satisfactory, they were then put on piecework, and could make about two dollars and a half a week, to start.

Nell was led up narrow dark stairs to the top floor, where the inside cubbyhole rooms were so dark that the girls worked from seven o'clock in the morning until six at night by gaslight. She saw girls as young as twelve among them, pale as ghosts, consumptive-looking and underfed. The girls were locked in during working hours, so that even had there been adequate fire escapes, and there were not, there would have been no exit in case of fire.

And yet, the girls told Nell as she worked beside them making innumerable box lids, conditions in this factory were far better than in others they had worked in in Yonkers and Brooklyn. One girl, who had been there many years, made eleven dollars a week. Some could earn five and six on piecework. Of course, they admitted, girls were often taken on for the two weeks' tryout without wages, and dismissed at the end of that period.

The worst employers, Nell learned, were women immigrants, who thought nothing of working the girls twelve hours a day and paying them thirty-five cents a week. She learned, too, of rackets in connection with factory and sweatshop work—advertisements in newspapers offering at a price to teach girls knitting and fine embroidery which would guarantee them "steady work" in good-paying jobs. But the girls who answered such advertisements, and Nell verified their claims in later personal experience stories, found themselves plucked of their hard-earned savings and taught nothing at all.

While many of the girls lived in tenements with their parents, the whole family pooling wages to pay for rent, food, and clothing and in this way surviving during the long stretches of unemployment the various members were sure to encounter, some of them roomed together. The girls avoided the "Homes for Females" as the plague. These, they told Nell, were often fraudulently run and were homes in name only, as Nell well knew.

In her turn Nell told the girls of the Cooper Institute and the free school there. She urged them to try and better their lots through education and discussion. But, in spite of her strange advanced ideas, the girls accepted Nell as one of them, and Nell paid a nice tribute to them in her writings. "Factories as they now exist are totally unfit places for women," she concluded one article. "There is only one advantage in being a factory girl. Their manners are so polite and they dress so neatly that it is not unusual for men to offer seats to them rather than to the more fashionable ladies on the stagecars. I have seen in high positions many worse girls than the white slaves of New York."

Nell now turned her attention to politics. She leveled an attack at New York's notorious lobby king, Edward R. Phelps. Though he had been suspected of crookedness for years, it was not until Nell went to work on him that he was brought low. On April 1, 1888, she began her exposé in this Bly fashion:

> For I'm a pirate King!
> I'm in the lobby ring!
> Oh! What an uproarious
> Jolly and glorious
> Biz for a pirate king.

"I was a Lobbyist last week. I went up to Albany to watch a professional briber in the act. The briber, Lobbyist, and boodler whom I caught was Mr. Ed Phelps. He calls himself 'King of the Lobby.' I pretended I wanted to have him help me kill a certain bill."

118

Nell met Phelps, a flashily dressed man of about forty-five, in Albany's Kenmore Hotel. Though at first his manner was wary, he was soon convinced Nell was "an honest innocent female in need of his assistance." Nell had selected Bill 191 to be "killed," and told Phelps that, if it passed, it would ruin her husband's patent-medicine business. She added, hesitantly, she was willing to pay up to two thousand dollars to have the bill disposed of. That did it!

The lobby king, with a gleam in his eye, told Nell he could not only get the bill killed for her, but could do it at a bargain rate. He showed Nell the names of twelve men in the New York State Assembly and said he could "buy" at least six of them without any trouble.

"I can get the lot for one thousand dollars," he told Nell. "Mr. Crosby of New York is a rich man and not for sale," he went on calmly, "but we can buy—" and he mentioned the names of the "available assemblymen."

After some preliminary arrangements, Nell promised to meet Phelps in his New York office on the following Friday. When she appeared there he told her to write a check to a relative of his, named Cheesborough, and the deal would be clinched. Nell asked him for a receipt, then she pretended to discover she had by accident left her checkbook in her hotel room. Phelps agreed to meet her at the Hotel St. James in half an hour. She managed to rush out carrying the receipt, and went directly to the *World* office while another reporter was sent to the St. James to watch Phelps.

On schedule the lobby king and his son appeared at the hotel. They strolled around a while, watching for Nell, before repairing to the nearby Delmonico Restaurant. Then they returned to the hotel and cooled their heels several hours more.

It was not until Phelps was indicted that he met Nell again.

With the receipt as evidence, he was forced to admit his deal with her. On the basis of her exposé, there was legislative investigation. Soon Albany was minus its most powerful lobby king, and the public demanded and got more honest politicians in the New York Legislature for some years to come.

Early in her career Nell had written about city prisons, and she returned to this theme again in one of her next stories, called, "Why Don't Women Reform?" In describing the pathetic creatures she saw in a female ward, Nell wrote: "The pencil of Doré might have gotten a sketch of Hades from just such a scene—so lost and hopeless." Again Nell had asked why? Girl after girl told her the same story— old woman after old woman. Drink, bad associations, and harsh treatment at the hands of society had brought them there.

"What started me off?" a gray-eyed girl in black straw hat with bright red roses on it repeated her question. "The same thing that brings all the others. Despair. I lost my husband and then an only child of eight. So began drinking. And once the police know you are on the town, they go after you, drunk or sober."

"Why did you leave home?" Nell asked another "fallen woman," a hardened regular though still in her teens.

"My parents were too strict with me," she told Nell. "They wouldn't let me have any fun. I went to a ball one night and my father beat me for it. I ran away. Parents drive their children from home by being too harsh."

"You're still young—you can reform," Nell urged her.

"Don't turn missionary on me," the girl replied, then added bitterly, "Why don't police pull the men in? Why don't they protect us and go after the *men?*"

Nell wondered that too.

"What made the greatest impression on me as I visited our city jails?" Nell wrote. "First, the utter uselessness of the unenlightened form of punishment now meted out; second, that most of the misery of the women there comes from cheap drinks."

It was in February of 1889 that Nell had her second encounter with amiable Judge Duffy, who had turned her over to the Bellevue authorities more than two years before as an insane girl. The circumstances of their reunion were almost as bizarre as those of the first time. Deciding to test the truth of stories she had heard about the ease with which innocent women could be arrested and kept in jail, Nell and a woman friend concocted a tale of having become acquainted with each other on the train from Albany, N.Y. They registered at the Gedney House and Nell's companion then charged Nell with taking two fifty-dollar bills from her purse. It didn't take long for a house detective to arrive and march Nell to court, where her accuser, giving the fictitious name of "Miss Peters," painted a black picture of her guilt.

"What's *your* name?" the night sergeant asked Nell gruffly.

"Must I tell?" she demurred.

The detective who had brought her in whispered, "Say Jane Smith—give some name—or it will go hard with you."

Nell said "Jane Smith," and was led through a gate to a cubicle of a room to be searched. As she disrobed, she saw curious male eyes peering at her through a crack in the door. Furious but helpless, she had to submit to a frisking. Then she was taken to the jail.

She followed a jailer past a cell where a drunken man called after her, past another occupied by a pale-faced woman who laughed at her. She heard abusive conversations between men and women prisoners shouted from cell to cell. She was placed in a cell of her own. It had a brass faucet for water, a tin cup, a bed composed of a board fastened to the wall about two feet off the floor. There was no pillow or covering of any kind, but, as Nell folded her jacket for a headrest and wrapped herself in her silk circular cape, a good-natured turnkey appeared with a comforter. She thanked him, and he stayed and entertained her with tales of horror to help pass the time. One of the finest girls he'd ever seen, he told Nell, had died of heart failure in this very cell. Another had hanged herself.

"We've had babies born in here too," he concluded. "Now I must make my rounds. Try and rest. You'll need it. And if you want to pay for a cup of coffee, I'll have one sent in to you in the morning."

Early next morning, a new jailer appeared."Hello, Birdie,

are you awake?" he asked Nell. "Give me that tin cup."

His appearance was the signal for much conversation. As Nell listened in dismayed astonishment, one woman yelled, "Hello, Petie. Judge Duffy's on today, and *he's* all right. Know what'll happen? I'll put my bangs back and he'll say, 'Well, Mamie, they charged you with being drunk and disorderly again.' Then I'll say 'To —— with it!' and Duffy'll say, 'Ten days or ten dollars.' I'll say, 'I haven't a —— cent.' And then I'll get free board and lodging as usual."

The conversations became even stronger, and Nell was glad when the detective appeared and took her over to the Jefferson Market Court, though she had her doubts about the reception Judge Duffy would give her this time.

While awaiting his arrival, she was put in a large cell with twenty unkempt, foul-mouthed women in various stages of intoxication. When the detective reappeared, he had another man with him.

"Miss Smith," the man began, "I am a runner for Lawyer McClelland. As your case is going dead against you, I thought you would like to have some advice. If you retain me, I will run to McClelland's house and he will come and fix things. McClelland's a politician and has a pull with the officers and the judges. Shall I get him for you?"

Nell surveyed the "Tammany boy" and said virtuously, "I don't think I'll need that. I am innocent, so I'm not afraid."

He shook his head sadly. "They have got a case against you for sure. The woman whose money is missing is out there with two witnesses. But you give me ten dollars and McClelland will make everything all right."

"I'll think it over," said Nell, a glint in her eye.

"If you don't," he threatened, "I'll be out there beside you and I'll see that you're put under a thousand dollars' bail. The Grand Jury will get you then."

This illuminating talk was interrupted when the detective took Nell before "the little judge whose kind heart is ever with the unfortunate," as she wrote later. As the long sad tale about Nell's depravity was unfolded, Judge Duffy sat looking at her with a puzzled expression.

"Lift your veil," he said, as if trying to recollect something.

Remembering a time before when he had said the same words, Nell did so, and was barely able to conceal her relief when he did not recognize her. The judge had passed on thousands of cases since then and, though he seemed trying to recall her, he could not.

"This girl hasn't the face of a thief," he said goodnaturedly. "I have seen lots of thieves and she hasn't the look of one. Where is the woman who made this charge?"

"She promised to be here," said the detective nervously, "but she hasn't appeared yet."

"She's probably found her money then." The judge beamed on Nell. "You remind me of someone. My sister."

That again, too! Nell tried not to laugh as he turned to the detective. "I don't believe this lady stole anything. She is discharged!"

So much for the runner's threats, thought Nell. But, as

she started to leave the station house, the detective pursued her. He reminded her it was his influence on the judge that had gotten her off so lightly and invited her to repay his kindness by going out to dinner with him.

"It's impossible. I have to hurry now," said Nell coyly.

He persisted. This, he told Nell, might be the beginning of a beautiful friendship.

"At least let me hear from you," he begged.

"You'll hear from me, one of these days," smiled Nell and went her way.

She returned to the *World* and wrote her story. Judge Duffy must have read it with mixed emotions. But the turnkey and detective would have been even more astonished. For, though Nell strongly advocated that women searchers be employed in station houses and that male officers be given no opportunity for frisking the ladies or squinting at them through peepholes, and though she emphatically urged the segregation of male and female prisoners, she added:

"Innocent women falling into the hands of police are not necessarily badly treated. If all the turnkeys are as kind as the one I encountered, no women could ever fill their places. Women grow harder from daily contact with crime, and are seldom kind to their unfortunate sisters. There is no sympathy left in them. Men, whatever their failings, stay human. That is true of Judge Duffy. Even detectives, though subject to erring, are human, though I do not think they should be tempted by being given sole custody of a female prisoner."

Nell got her women searchers in station houses, along with other improvements.

By the middle of 1889, the wheels of reform Nellie Bly had set in motion in Pittsburg were whirling merrily in New York City. Nell visited the city dispensaries and disclosed how simple it was for people who could well afford to pay to secure free services which should belong only to the deserving needy. Simply by declaring that her throat bothered her, she found herself ushered into the office of a throat specialist who advised clipping off part of her tonsils. He brought out his murderous-looking shears and would have done this at once, for it was the custom in this era to make short work of tonsils without benefit of anesthetics. Nell, however, objected, and went her way to write a report, taking her tonsils with her.

She was greatly impressed, however, by the many hardworking self-sacrificing physicians who received little or no pay for their charitable service. She took their part and helped secure better salaries and public support for their work.

She visited diet kitchens and wrote of what must be done to feed undernourished children. And she climbed countless flights of filthy stairs, to bring aid and comfort to the blind, the crippled, the sick, and the dying tenement women, all the sufferers who besieged the *World* for her help.

"For God's sake, send Nellie Bly. She can do anything," they pleaded. And Nellie responded. She risked yellow fever, malaria, and cholera in sweltering pestholes during summer and tuberculosis and diphtheria during winter to focus attention on the need for improving the terrible housing conditions in New York.

"We keep pouring more and more unassimilated into our cities," said the *World,* "so that Tammany will have more votes. It is deplorable."

Deplorable it was, but it was only one of many situations Nellie Bly was determined to correct. Her exposés for the *World* not only took her into every corner of New York but to other cities as well. She was intent on revealing unfair practices everywhere.

Her sex, rather than remaining a liability in her work, now became a shield for her. In spite of the fact that she had gained wide publicity on her asylum story, for several years no photographs were published of her. She aroused the curiosity of readers at all levels. A young woman wrote to her on May 27, 1887:

> We girls think you are just too lovely for anything. It must be perfectly beautiful to go around just as you please and to catch all the bad people.
>
> Please won't you tell me if you are a man or a woman? My husband's brother says you never existed at all and I say you are a girl. Please decide for us. Inclosed find stamp for reply.
>
> P.S. Do you play tennis?

Some editors of rival papers refused to believe she was a pretty young girl or even a woman at all. They disputed her very existence and insisted the romantic name covered the activities of a group of brilliant male reporters.

Even the racketeers, sweatshop proprietors, and shady politicians who lived in terror of an invincible Nellie Bly coming disguised into their lives were never prepared for the girl who finally did appear to mete out justice to them. For Nell's principal disguise was her brilliant personality.

"*You* can't be Nellie Bly," people told her in astonishment when they learned her identity. "Why, Nellie Bly must have had a lifetime of experience!"

Yes, a lifetime of experience had been hers, Nellie thought, recalling the places she had been, the things she had seen, the many kinds of people she had known in the few short years since she stood first beside George Madden's desk. A long lifetime. *And she was not yet twenty-two years old.*

CHAPTER XIII

THE BRIGHTER SIDE

But there was a side to Nellie Bly's nature that was very gay and her love of fun came bubbling to the surface. Between weightier matters she took her public into her confidence about her more frivolous activities. She could make fascinating stories out of these, too.

She had her readers with her through her adventures in the blizzard of 1888 and even told them about the morning when she slipped on the icy pavement and, with a cry of "Good-by, perpendicular!" went sprawling. She mentioned in some detail a handsome violet-eyed stranger. He came to her rescue, brushed her off, and sent her on her way again in pursuit of a petty mendicant known as a "bread-crust dropper." This shabby individual slyly scattered bits of dry bread, waited for a passer-by, and then pounced upon a scrap and pretended to eat it, creating sympathy for his starving condition. That the rescuer had been James Metcalfe, editor of *Life* and a man destined to be of importance to her neither she nor the public knew then.

She took her readers for a series of madcap adventures in Central Park in the spring as she investigated troublesome "mashers." She reported on some colorful personalities. The prince of all mashers, she discovered, was a bartender who, on his day off, appeared in the park in a carriage with fine horses, his mustache waxed for conquest, ready to snare the ladies with tales of being richer and more sporty than Diamond Jim Brady himself. No gay gentleman driving through the park dared wink at a girl after that, for fear she'd turn out to be Nellie Bly.

When she grew tired of New York City, Nell drove her own horse and buggy through Oneida County, the hop country. She described the farms with hops planted in straight rows like corn, the aroma from the kilns, and she told delightedly of the hoppickers who sang as they worked:

> Say you love me, Mollie darling
> Say you love none else but me.

She revealed that the native pickers feared the Italians brought in from New York City to compete with them and undercut wages, but that the whole community, homespun citizens, Indians, and Italians, joined in the fun at a hop dance. Nellie went to it too, sat on a big yellow pumpkin in a lantern-decorated barn, and kept time to the music of three fiddles, an accordion, and a mouth organ.

"Ladies and gents," the caller would yell, "please form the Money Musk. This way—step up smartly. Tee dumel, de dum, ah rattied de lum—whirl!"

Finally Nellie too flung herself into the dance and round and round the shadowy hall the readers whirled with her.

World readers went with Nellie behind the scenes of Buffalo Bill's Wild West Show one hot summer day. In the mosquito-filled tent she introduced them to Bill himself, with his precise English accent, and gave them an account of his daredevil riders.

One of Nell's most sparkling stories let them in on her own stage experience when she decided to become a show girl. She found among the *World's* advertisements a call for a hundred show girls for a spectacular pantomime. She rushed to the Academy of Music and was promptly hired and told to appear at seven that evening. She came through the stage entrance on the dot.

"You're an Amazon," the stage manager told her. "Here's your costume. Get ready."

"Do I go on without any rehearsal?" Nell asked in surprise.

"No time for that. Walk between girls who know the routine and they will tell you what to do."

But the regulars eyed the newcomers coldly in the crowded dressing room. Everyone was trying to get into tights. The girl who was having the least luck was a modest miss who thought it could be done without taking off her high button shoes! When they all were finally dressed and equipped with shields and spears they appeared to Nell very defeated Amazons, to say the least.

"My garments were too big," Nell wrote, "my ballet slippers four sizes too long. I put rouge on my face, then found I had forgotten my powder. My white wig was so small my own dark hair showed underneath it. The helmet was so large it kept slipping back on my head. I was a sad sight!"

But the show must go on! Nell heard the call, "On stage," and rushed down the stairs in a tangle of spears and armor. She saw a blaze of gaslight, heard a crash of music, and with an inward laugh at her boldness faced a New York audience in the Amazon march.

"You started with the wrong foot," the girl on one side of her whispered. Nell corrected that.

"You've got your shield on the wrong arm," came from the other side. Nell was about to correct that, too, when the order came, "Face about." Nell faced left and discovered everyone else had turned right.

Since she couldn't go backward while the rest went forward, Nell switched around. As the girls marched across the stage, she changed her shield and poised her spear at her side. Now she was in order. Again the row of Amazons moved toward the footlights. There was a whispered "Stand still." Nell stood.

But a voice came from the wings this time and it was no whisper.

"What the — blazes went wrong?"

"I knew," Nell finished her story. "The other girls had marched to the side of the stage and divided. I was left standing in the center of the stage, all alone. With more haste than grace, I ran after them, thankful to get away from it all.

"I am out of a stage engagement at present," she added.

Scorned by the theater, Nellie turned to more dignified pursuits. She decided to write a story about America's First Ladies. In addition to Mrs. Grover Cleveland, then mistress

NELLIE BLY ON THE STAGE.

SHE WEARS A SCANT COSTUME AND MARCHES WITH THE AMAZONS.

It Isn't Very Hard to Get Such a Job—The Girls Earn $5 a Week—Tights that Did Not Fit—Dressing in a Crowded Room— How She Behaved on the Stage—A Bad Beginning.

I MADE my début as a chorus girl or stage Amazon last week. It was my first appearance on any stage and came about through reading among THE WORLD advertisements one that called for 100 girls for a spectacular pantomime, so I found myself one afternoon at the stage door of the Academy of Music. There were but two men there. I looked at them and they looked at me, and as nobody made any movement to speak, I asked:

"Where do I go in answer to the advertisement?"

133

of the White House, there were living seven women, five of them widows of Presidents, who had formerly lived there. They formed a link between Civil War days and the close of the Victorian era: Mrs. John Tyler, Mrs. James K. Polk, Mrs. Harriet Johnson, the niece of James Buchanan, Mrs. Ulysses S. Grant, Mrs. Rutherford B. Hayes, Mrs. James A. Garfield, Mrs. John McElroy, sister of Chester A. Arthur, and Mrs. Cleveland, wife of the President. Nell frowned over the list of widows and the toll the presidency took.

With the exception of the President's wife, not one of the ladies now lived in Washington.

"Mrs. Tyler travels a great deal and visits among her children," Nellie Bly reported. "She is a descendant of the first white child born of British parents in New York State, and the child of the first white child born in Connecticut. She met President Tyler in Washington at a grand reception while her father was Secretary of State there; he was thirty-five years older than she. The night he proposed she wore a white tarleton gown and a crimson Grecian cap. He gave her a song he had composed in her honor, 'Sweet Lady, Awake!' They were married in the Church of the Ascension in New York."

Nell next called on bright-eyed Mrs. Polk in Nashville, Tennessee, and sat with her in her comfortable parlor with its rosewood furniture and maroon plush upholstery and listened to the stories of the past. When she had been in Washington, wine had been served only at state dinners and there was no dancing. But in spite of that they managed to have fun, the old lady admitted, her eyes twinkling.

"I shall never forget when I opened the Cincinnati exhibition," she told Nell. "I touched a little button and set in motion machinery miles away. One young man said to me, 'Mrs. Polk, we will never let you down. When nature gives out, we will keep you up with electricity!' How rapidly the world is advancing! I like to keep up with it and I shall as long as I live."

In spite of her age, Mrs. Polk could still read with the aid of a magnifying glass. She was a Presbyterian and said she never skipped communion service.

"I have never been back to Washington once," she confided, "and I have never missed it."

In search of Mrs. Cleveland, Nellie Bly arrived in the capital and drove along dusty roads to Oak View, the President's summer home, in a rented carriage. The house looked pretty, she thought, its red roof flashing in the sunshine. But she was surprised that the grounds showed little care.

Nell had come unannounced. As her victoria drove up she saw a small dachshund curled up on one end of the veranda and a large dog on the other, as though they both stood watch over a beautiful woman resting in the hammock. But the noise of the wheels startled them all. The dogs barked and the lovely lady sprang up and disappeared.

A boy came to the door when Nell rang the bell. He led her to the parlor, put the letter of introduction she gave him on a silver salver, and went away with it. From where Nell sat she could peek about the house. It was richly furnished,

135

with fine rugs on the hardwood floors, brocades at the windows. A life-sized crayon portrait of President Cleveland hung in the hall and a bust of him flanked by a pair of candles stood on the parlor center table. They were very impressive and they were as much of the presidential pair as Nell was to see. The boy returned almost at once and said that President Cleveland did not believe it good policy for Mrs. Cleveland to be interviewed.

Nell knew that the First Lady attended few receptions and had only a small circle of intimate friends. She went back to New York grateful that she was a journalist and did not have to enact the role of bird in a gilded cage.

She found a visit with the widow of U. S. Grant a very different matter. Mrs. Grant's life had been crammed with wonderful experiences and she loved to talk about them. After her husband had served two terms as President and retired from politics, they had made a tour of foreign countries, and Mrs. Grant had been received like a queen in all of them. But she remembered the eight years in the White House as the happiest in her life, and she said she had cried when she left.

"Ulysses and I enjoyed the receptions and all that went with them," she chuckled. "*Harper's* used to publish cartoons of 'Grant's House on Reception Day.' They pictured ladies sitting on curbstones pulling on their slippers, and the entrance jammed and people tumbling out of windows. The White House had no terrors for me. I think self-forgetfulness is death to fear."

Mrs. Grant had showed no fear of the White House interior decoration she inherited. "Imagine a green lounge and a clashing blue chair on a shabby carpet with roses as big as washbowls! I tell you, I worked to put that place in order."

Mrs. Grant was a Southerner and had been given six slaves as a wedding present, but she stood by her husband stanchly during the Civil War. She had never doubted he would win it, she declared, and never believed he would lose his life in battle. She followed him to Memphis to be near him. When the troops were ordered into battle, Grant said to her, "If Lee surrenders I will return and we will go to Washington together. If he takes to the mountains, make your way back home as you can; you will have to go it alone." But she said, "I won't go it alone. I'll wait for you!" And she did.

Nell spoke of General Grant's memoirs, which he had written just before his death. His wife's eyes filled with tears.

"If it hadn't been for that book I'd have been left penniless," she said. "The General never was a business success. He was too honest, and he would not believe anyone else could cheat him. This house belonged to me and the General was persuaded to mortgage it and invest the money. He lost everything—we had eighty-four dollars in the world! The General was ill but determined to leave me provided for. It broke my heart to watch him, struggling to finish that book. But he did it. Proceeds from it paid off a mortgage of $56,000 and interest and I paid all the General's debts. I knew he would have wanted me to do that."

Mrs. Grant smiled proudly. "Writing that book was the greatest battle the General ever fought."

When Nell had exhausted the story possibilities in the wives of the famous, she turned to famous women themselves. The suffragettes in America had advanced their cause tremendously. They had not yet succeeded in winning the right to vote, but they were putting up a candidate for President just the same, a woman candidate, for the second time. Oblivious to male jeers, catcalls, and the throwing of overripe tomatoes, they marched with stirring songs and banners flying in support of Belva Lockwood.

Nell did not join the parades. But she went to interview Mrs. Lockwood. The presidential candidate had come to New York from Washington to lecture and was staying in a fashionable suite at 126 West Twenty-third Street.

While Nellie waited to see her, she noted some portraits of Lillian Russell in various poses. The popular actress had recently taken to wearing bloomers for tricycle riding at her Manhasset, Long Island, home and it had made her very popular with the suffragettes. Miss Russell was popular with the public too. Nell wondered if she might not have more chance of being elected to office than the very capable Belva.

Mrs. Lockwood proved to be a gray-haired woman who wore black-rimmed eyeglasses. She had a lecture platform manner and was quite austere, but Nell liked her and they talked as one emancipated woman to another.

"Do you truly expect to be elected President?" Nell asked bluntly.

"Certainly."

"This is the second time you have been nominated, isn't it?"

"Yes. But I was ill in Washington the first time."

"I suppose you depend entirely on the votes of men to put you in office?" Nell asked, and Mrs. Lockwood smiled.

"Until women have the vote. All thinking people know they will have it eventually. Even President Cleveland told me the other day, 'It has to come; we all recognize that.'"

"Have you any newspapers backing you?"

"No. There is nothing to make it worth their while yet. And of course we get no help from the other parties. But we have private backers who believe in our cause."

"If you do not reach the White House, what good will come of your campaign?"

"It educates the people to the idea. We must work, not just talk. Men say, 'Let's see what you can do.' We must show them."

"Do all women support you?"

"Thinking women and working women do. Society women never go outside of society. The very poor, the masses, are no better. One is the doll, the other the slave." Belva Lockwood waved them aside with an eloquent gesture of her hand. "We shall win without them, one day."

Mrs. Lockwood had seen progress. Like her husband, she was an attorney. She had worked her way through law school and had been admitted to the bar in spite of strong prejudice against women there.

"People are less wedded to party today," she said. "They do their own thinking."

"What do you think of Harrison's chances?" Nell asked her.

"Well, if you can win by handshaking. . . ."

"And President Cleveland's?"

Belva Lockwood rose to this question like a true suffragette.

"Why, he's not the candidate. Mrs. Cleveland is."

"You have been interested in so many projects, Mrs. Lockwood," Nell said, "what is the one most important to you now?"

Belva Lockwood's enthusiasm made her look truly beautiful.

"I am interested in trying to establish a court of international arbitration between America and foreign countries. I am beginning with France. Other nations will follow."

Nellie Bly came out into the sunshine thinking hard. While she fought her individual battle for a place in the sun, these women were fighting a universal one. They were dreaming impossible dreams, they were told. But today's realities were the impossible dreams of only a few years ago. One day women journalists would be taken for granted on every newspaper; women voters would go to the polls as a matter of course. The world was moving ahead and Nellie was watching it happen.

CHAPTER XIV

AROUND THE WORLD—BON VOYAGE!

But although the world advanced steadily in some departments, it did not do so fast enough in others to suit the *World's* girl reporter. It was still a universe of slow trains, unseaworthy steamers, bad transportation, and worse communication. Nellie Bly's great-uncle, Thomas Kennedy, had circumnavigated the globe, but it had taken him three years to do it and his health had been so shattered he had died before he could write the book about it he had intended.

Nell had often wished she could have traveled with him, however. One of her favorite books was one written in 1872 by Jules Verne, the famous French writer, *Around the World in Eighty Days.* In it Phineas Fogg, the English hero of the tale, raced against time to win a bet and set this incredible speed record. The achievement remained wholly in the realm of fancy, along with a trip to the moon about which Verne also wrote. But the book was a popular favorite and challenged the public imagination.

It challenged Nellie Bly specifically one Sunday evening. She now lived in an uptown flat with her mother. She had been restlessly pacing the floor of her room, thinking up story ideas to submit to the editor on Monday. She was

brain weary, for she had worked long hours without vacation since coming on the *World* staff. Finally she slumped
discouragedly into a chair.

"Oh, I wish I were at the ends of the earth!" she said
out loud. An answer came as clearly to her as though it had
been spoken aloud too.

"Then why don't you go there?"

"Too far—takes too long."

"Make the trip in a hurry. See how quickly you can do it,"
the startling dialogue with herself continued.

How fast *could* anyone go? she wondered. She began to
think about it. She went to her bookshelf and pulled out
the Jules Verne story. It had been fantasy in 1872. But there
had been improvements since then. What would a real
race against time show now? Could anyone challenge
Fogg's record? Did *she* dare?

She took the idea to Jules Chambers, who was now her
managing editor. But he felt that Nellie Bly was at last
overreaching herself and said so. For more than a year,
needled by inquiries from readers, the *World* had been
toying with the idea of sending a man around the globe
to investigate travel facilities. But, because of the slowness
of international mail service and poor cable facilities in
many places, they had shelved the project. Chambers finally agreed to discuss Nell's proposal with the business office.
They too vetoed it.

"You are a woman and would need protection in foreign
countries," she was reminded.

"I have traveled in a foreign country without protection," Nell reminded them.

"A woman has to carry so much baggage. It would slow you down."

"I will travel light."

The *World* officials were not convinced.

"If we send anyone, it will be a man."

"The day you do that," Nell told them, "I will start on the trip for another newspaper."

But she could get no definite promise. While she collected all the travel information she could lay hands on, just in case, she went ahead with more prosaic assignments and the *World* went ahead with plans for laying the cornerstone of the new Pulitzer Building at 56-63 Park Row. Joseph Pulitzer's eyesight had failed completely. He came to the office only occasionally now, and he was never to see except in his mind's eye the home for the *World* he had dreamed of. But it would soon be a reality.

On October 10, 1889, along with many other celebrities, including forty-two-year-old Thomas Edison, whose invention of an incandescent electric lamp some years before had startled the nation, Nell attended the dedicatory ceremonies.

It was not until November that she was hastily summoned to a meeting with Editor Chambers and Business Manager J. W. Turner.

"Could you be ready to start on a trip around the world in a day and a half?" Mr. Chambers asked her.

"I could be ready in a minute and a half," replied the ecstatic Nell. "Do I race against anyone?"

"You race against time."

"Against Phineas Fogg's time?"

"You can't beat that, of course——"

"I can try," said Nell.

"You'll need a traveling costume. And you can take only a small bag——"

"Don't worry. I'll get my equipment. When I want things done at the last minute, the way I always do, and I get the reply, 'It's too late. I hardly think it can be done,' I say, 'Nonsense! If you want to do it, you can do it.' The question is 'Do you want to do it?' People respond to this—I get what I'm after."

She whipped out of the *World* office, veil aflutter as usual, and went directly to the fashionable dressmaking establishment of William Ghormley on East Nineteenth Street.

"I must have a dress by evening," she announced. It was to be a blue broadcloth dress that would hold up under constant wear. She got it, fittings, bustle, bones and all, and a smart camel's hair coat, a double-peaked ghillie cap, and a satchel as well. The satchel she packed with great care. It contained two more ghillie caps, three veils, a pair of slippers, toilet articles, an inkstand, pens, pencils, copy paper, needles, thread, a dressing gown, tennis blazer, a flask and drinking cup, several changes of flannel underwear, handkerchiefs, fresh ruchings, a jar of cold cream, and a lightweight silk bodice. She could barely lock the bag.

Her silk waterproof she would have to carry on her arm.

She put in her pocket one twenty-four-hour watch, set to New York time, and wore on her wrist another to record local times.

THE TWENTY-FOUR-HOUR WATCH.

Courtesy of The New York Public Library,
New York City

The next morning she was assigned Passport No. 247 and collected two hundred pounds in English gold and Bank of England notes. She also took along American gold and paper money to use as a test of the extent American currency was known outside the country. She carried her papers and valuables in a chamois bag hung around her neck. She was advised to carry a pistol for protection, but the memory of her Mexican cavalier reassured her.

"There will be gentlemen wherever I go," she said. "Whether they are French, English, German, or American will make little difference. They will protect me."

But on her left hand she wore her thumb ring, the lucky talisman of her first *World* assignment.

In a costume which was to make history and be pictured down the century, Nellie Bly went by horse-drawn stage to the Christopher Street Ferry and crossed to the Jersey side of the Hudson River. At nine-forty and six seconds o'clock on November 14 she set sail on the Hamburg steamer *Augusta Victoria*. Her mother stood on the wharf wiping tears from behind her spectacles and friends and newspaper associates worriedly waved her good-by and good luck.

Nell, with the *World's* assistance, had mapped out a rough itinerary and a code which she would use to report her progress. She had promised to be back in the *World* office in seventy-five days. No one there believed it would be possible to do it in that time, or even in eighty-five. She was starting out in a season of storms and typhoons at sea, and with no positive knowledge as to sailing dates anywhere.

Her schedule called for her to be in London on November 21, Paris the twenty-third, Brindisi, Italy, the twenty-fifth, the Suez on the twenty-seventh, Ceylon on December 10, Singapore December 19, Christmas in Hong Kong, Yokohama January 7, San Francisco the twenty-second, and back in the *World* office on January 27. But there was doubt as to whether the mail train she was scheduled to take to Brindisi left every Friday night or only occasionally. Nor did anyone know exactly when a ship for India or China was due to sail from there.

Nell herself, though she had seemed blithely optimistic when she talked to reporters before sailing, had many misgivings. She had never been to sea before and she had been told all kinds of horror tales about shipwrecks, fevers, and the shanghaiing of foreigners. As she waved good-by to America and the *Augusta Victoria* moved slowly down the windy bay, her heart sank. "I'm off," she thought. "But shall I ever get back?"

The editor had told her that the day before her trip was decided he had had a dream. In it Nell came to him and told him she was going to run a race. Doubting her ability as a runner, he turned his back so as not to see the finish. He heard the band play and the applause and then she came to him with tears in her eyes and said, "I lost the race."

It was small wonder when she proceeded to get seasick her first day out, and a male passenger said laughingly,"And she's going around the world alone!" Nell reached a low point, for her. Captain Abers told her the only way to conquer seasickness was to eat, but as night came on and the ship tossed roughly about, Nell felt less and less inclined toward food. One of the few other women on board refused to undress for the night. If the ship went down, as she was sure it would, she intended to be respectably clothed. Nell crawled off to bed in misery "to dream dreadful dreams."

...US AND HUMOROUS
RECIPES
ARE RECEIVED DAILY BY
THE EVENING WORLD
TO KEEP
A Husband
AT HOME IN THE EVENING.

Che

CIRCULATION GUARANTEED
GREATER THAN THAT OF ANY TWO OTHER
AMERICAN NEWSPAPERS COMBINED.

CIRCUL

VOL. XXX., NO. 10,313.　　　　12 PAGES.　　　　NE

AROUND THE WORLD,

A Continuous Trip Which Will Girdle the Spinning Globe.

Nellie Bly to Make an Unequalled Rapid-Transit Record.

NOW, 30,000 MILES IN A RUSH!

Can Jules Verne's Great Dream Be Reduced to Actual Fact?

A VERITABLE FEMININE PHINEAS FOGG.

On a Four-Day Notice Miss Bly Starts Out with a Gripsack for the Longest Journey Known to Mankind—She Knows No Such Word as Fail, and Will Add Another to Her List of Triumphs—Circumnavigators of Other Days—Speed of Existing Lines of Travel to Be Tested—How the Idea Was Suggested — Judge Daly on "The World's" New Enterprise—Will the Imaginary Record of Eighty Days Be Beaten?

THE WORLD to-day undertakes the task of turning a dream into a reality. Thousands upon thousands have read with interest the imaginary journey which Jules Verne, that prince of dreamers, sent his hero, Phineas Fogg, on, when he undertook to win a wager by circumnavigating this globe within the limit of Eighty Days. Thousands upon thousands have been content to stop with the reading and curiously enough not one seems to have carried out the idea of doing it, and it remains for THE WORLD to lead the way in this as in so many other paths. To-day at 9.30 o'clock Nellie Bly, so well known to the millions who have read of her doings, as told by her captivating pen, will set out as a Female Phineas Fogg, and, if nothing prevents

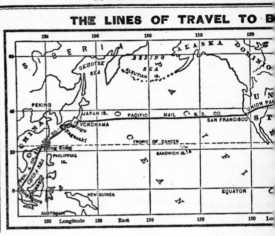

THE LINES OF TRAVEL TO B

NELLIE BLY.

Nellie's schedule called for her to b in London on November 21, Paris the twenty-third, Brindisi, Italy, the twenty-fifth, the Suez on the twenty seventh, Ceylon on December 10

World.

CIRCULATION PER DAY
DURING LAST 7 MONTHS, **340,167 COPIES.**

Fron

AVEN
DA

THURSDAY, NOVEMBER 14, 1889.　　　**12 PAGES.**

WED BY "THE WORLD'S" FLYING REPRESENTATIVE.

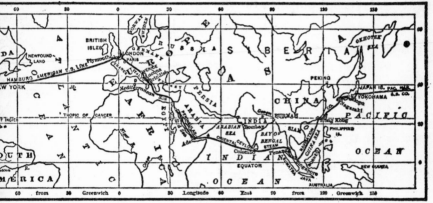

Courtesy of The New York Public Library, New York City

Singapore December 19, Christmas
in Hong Kong, Yokohama January 7,
San Francisco the twenty-second, and
back in the *World* office on January 27.

In New York the *World* broke the astonishing news to its readers that Nellie Bly had started on the first lap of a trip around the world to challenge the record of Jules Verne's hero, Phineas Fogg. The front page of November 15, 1889, trumpeted the story:

A CONTINUOUS TRIP WHICH WILL GIRDLE THE SPINNING GLOBE—NELLIE BLY TO MAKE AN UN-EQUALED RAPID-TRANSIT RECORD—NOW 30,000 MILES IN A RUSH—CAN JULES VERNE'S GREAT DREAM BE REDUCED BY ACTUAL FACT?

The World today undertakes the task of turning a dream into reality. . . . Nellie Bly, so well known to millions who have read of her doings, as told by her captivating pen, will set out as Female Phineas Fogg, and if nothing prevents and mishaps do not lengthen the line of her travel or the time taken in covering it, will report back to the office January 27, in seventy-five days. . . .

In imagination everyone will go with her.

Miss Bly starts off . . . by the Hamburg steamer *Augusta Victoria* with a gripsack, for the longest journey known to mankind. . . . She knows no such word as fail, and will add another to her list of triumphs—circumnavigation of the globe. . . . With all the millions now invested in methods and modes of communication, interstate and international, the story of Miss Bly will give a valuable pointer in enabling the reader to appreciate these avenues of intercourse at their full value, to see their merits and defects and note the present advanced state of invention in these lines of human effort.

So, with a map showing Nell's anticipated travel route, a personal interview with her as she set forth, "chic and pert in her double-peaked cap of light drab, showing not a wince of fear or trepidation," with items about past voyages of Magellan, Sir Francis Drake, Captain Cook, and other intrepid travelers, and with reassurance that modern steamers were amply supplied with chemists and laundry service, the *World* proceeded to stimulate reader interest in its usual flamboyant fashion. The editors could only hope, as they waited nervously for Nellie Bly's first cablegram and reports, that their lady of destiny would not let them down hard!

"We were afraid you were dead," Captain Abers told Nell in alarm. But she was very much alive. She had slept from seven o'clock the evening of November 14 until four in the afternoon of the fifteenth, and she felt wonderful. Although the sea was so rough that two sailors had been washed overboard during the night, and many people, including the man who laughed at her, were now violently ill, Nell had no more trouble. She felt like a veteran seaman. The sea air was invigorating, if extremely wet. Her appetite was good. She made friends easily and recorded their virtues and idiosyncrasies.

An American girl, the daughter of Carl Schurz, the publisher, was traveling to Germany, Nell wrote. She knew more than any man on board about politics, art, literature, or music, and besides she was very pretty. There was a man who took his pulse after every meal; another who counted the number of steps he took pacing the deck. There was a lively little terrier called "Home Sweet Home," nicknamed "Homie." There was the woman who slept in her clothes, and who kept pestering the Captain to turn back.

The Captain tried to keep the passengers from the discussion of shipwrecks and sea disasters by talking of other things, among them the erroneous impressions foreigners had of Americans. Many foreigners, he told them, did not even know where the United States was.

"Once there was delivered to my house in Hoboken a letter from a German, mailed to 'Captain Abers, First House in America.'" The Captain smiled. "I got the letter, too."

In spite of his efforts, the passengers knew it was one of the stormiest crossings in years. But six days and twenty-one hours after leaving New York, the *Augusta Victoria* docked in Southampton only slightly off schedule. All of the passengers stayed up to see Nell off on a tugboat at two-thirty in the morning. One gentleman offered to switch his plans and escort her to London, but she wouldn't hear of it. She could take care of herself. She was pleased, however, to be met by a London correspondent for the *World,* especially when he handed her a cablegram from M. and Mme. Jules Verne. It invited Nell to visit them in France, if she could possibly make it.

Nell was all excitement. "Oh I must see them! Can it be arranged?"

The reporter shook his head. "Not unless you go without sleep——"

"I wouldn't mind doing that. But how about connections?"

He looked dismal.

"All the regular trains for London have left. They may decide to run a special mail train. Otherwise we will have to stay here all night. In that case, seeing the Vernes will be completely out of the question."

But Nell gave a twist to her thumb ring and luck was with her. As they reached the Southampton wharf, they were informed that a passenger coach had been attached to a special mail train to accommodate passengers going into London.

Nell sent back to the *World* the detailed report of her Atlantic crossing, which was to reach them seventeen days later. Then she and the reporter were locked into her first English railroad carriage, along with a few other passengers. As they crawled toward London, Nell also got her first taste of European unheated, slow-motion transportation. And she still disliked being locked in. She tucked her icy feet against a foot warmer and asked her companion, "How should we get out of this train if it ran off the track?"

"Trains never run off the track in England," he told her proudly.

"No, too slow for that," she countered.

It was dawn when they reached London and passed through the almost deserted Waterloo Station. They rented a carriage and drove past Westminster Abbey and Buckingham Palace to the American Consulate, to pick up Nell's passport and credentials. Then they went to the London *World* headquarters.

"How do the streets back in the states compare with those of London?" the Englishman asked Nell.

"Not bad," she said, though she later wrote, "I saw shame-facedly how clean the London streets look in contrast with some I have seen in New York. But now that I was in foreign lands, I was determined to hear no word against my country."

At the *World* office, cables were waiting for Nell. She sent her first code message back home: "I'm all right—letter follows." She told them briefly of the hectic Atlantic trip and of her sudden decision to visit Jules Verne and then try to connect with the Brindisi mail train at Calais. Then she and her host had a breakfast of ham, eggs, and coffee and started out for Charing Cross Station.

As they arrived there the train for Folkstone and Boulogne pulled out, puffing and wheezing.

"That's a blasted shame," said her guide. "It's left early. You've missed the thing!"

But Nell took one horrified look and gathered up her skirts.

"I can't miss it," she screamed. "Run for it!" And she and the dignified Englishman sprinted after the rear coach.

CHAPTER XV

JULES VERNE—AND PHINEAS FOGG

WHAT the editors of the *World* thought when they received Nell's first cable telling of her change in plans, is not recorded. NELLIE BLY ON THE OTHER SIDE, they told their excited readers in front-page headlines on November 22. "The World's Globe Trotter Is in Southampton Today After a Tempestuous Voyage. May visit Jules Verne in France if she can do so without losing time."

The *World* wrote about Nell's mounting fan mail and the number of marriage proposals that were pouring in. It disclosed that the *City of Paris*, the steamer Nell had almost taken instead of the *Augusta Victoria*, had been greatly delayed by raging seas, and had nearly capsized. It discussed slow trains, bad connections, poor communications, and the mounting number of shipwrecks, preparing their readers for the worst. Then the editors chewed their copy pencils and waited, wondering what Nellie Bly would do next to increase their jitters.

But Nell had no time to worry about editors back home. She had caught the moving train at Charing Cross Station by an unladylike leap, thankful at the moment for English slowness. She had crossed the cold English Channel on a decrepit boat and gone without sleep for two nights, traveling 179½ miles out of her way for a visit with Jules Verne at Amiens, France. She knew that her race against time was just begun. Assured however, that she had at least three hours before the train left Amiens for Calais, where she hoped to catch the train to Brindisi, she made up her mind that this was one interview she had worked hard for and that she would enjoy it.

As the train pulled in only ten minutes late, Nell, hair tousled under her ghillie cap, nose smudged from train smoke, hurried down the Amiens platform with her gripsack. Jules Verne and Mme. Verne greeted her warmly. Accompanied by R. H. Sherard, a Paris journalist and interpreter, they had been pacing the station impatiently. Nell felt, as she shook hands with the incomparable writer and his lovely wife, that it was the most important meeting of her life, and tried to impress every detail of it on her mind.

Jules Verne, in turn, surveyed the smiling if travel-weary girl and said in French to his wife and interpreter, "Is it possible that this child is traveling around the world alone? Why, she is a mere baby." Amused, Nell took in every word.

She began to make notes too, mental ones. Jules Verne had brilliant black eyes, a white beard, and hair which fell in artistic disorder above his heavy brows. He walked with a slight limp. Mme. Verne was charming in appearance and manner, with a youthful face, though her hair was white too. She had a clear complexion and very red lips. She wore a watered-silk skirt and a sealskin jacket. On her head was a small velvet bonnet, and she carried a muff.

In a fine carriage Nell was whisked past bright shops and a park where nursemaids were pushing baby carriages. In less than twenty minutes they reached the Verne estate, shut off from the road by a high stone wall, and entered a large courtyard. They went up the steps of the fieldstone house and moved through a conservatory filled with blossoms into a large sitting room. Here there were hangings of soft velvet and several fine paintings on the walls. On the mantel were pieces of bronze statuary and a Louis Quinze clock. There were chairs in silk brocade and on one of them sat an Angora cat which Mme. Verne greeted with a stroke of her dainty hand.

In spite of her knowledge of French, Nell was self-conscious about her accent. She spoke through the interpreter. "Many of Monsieur Verne's books have American locales. Has Monsieur Verne been in America?" she asked.

Verne's expressive eyes filled with Gallic delight. "Once for a few days, during which I saw Niagara Falls. *Magnifique!*" He longed to return, he added, and had many letters from friends in the States, but his health these days prevented long journeys. He told Nell he once had owned a yacht and, though he had never set a speed record like his hero Fogg, he had traveled extensively searching for new scenes. Now, because of encroaching age, he was forced to forego this pleasure.

"What is your line of travel?" he asked Nell eagerly.

Nell rattled off her itinerary. "London, Calais, Brindisi,

Port Said, Ismailia, Suez, Aden, Colombo, Penang, Singapore, Hong Kong, Yokohama, San Francisco, and back in the *World* office January 27. That will be in just seventy-five days!" she said, cheeks flushed.

Jules Verne chuckled at her assurance and audacity. "But why do you not go to Bombay as Phineas Fogg did?"

Nell's eyes twinkled. "Because I am anxious to save time, not a young widow."

"You may save a young widower before you return," he countered.

Mme. Verne joined in the laughter and said mischievously that she hoped Nell would find a handsome husband on her tour. But Nell shook her head. She would be much too busy catching trains and boats from here on, she told them, to give thought to catching beaux.

Reminded that time was flying, Nell glanced at the Louis Quinze clock, compared it with her wrist watch, and saw that she must leave soon. There was only the one train she could take from here to Calais. The loss of it would mean a week's delay. If that happened, she might as well turn back.

She stood up and said to the interpreter, "Before I go, I should like so much to see Monsieur Verne's study."

"*Certainement,*" beamed Jules Verne.

He lit a tall wax candle and escorted her through the conservatory and up a winding spiral staircase. He opened a door off the hall and turned on a gas lamp.

"I had expected to see a hand-carved desk filled with trinkets," Nell wrote, "but I saw only a plain flat-topped

158

one. It was in a small room, modest and bare, with a single latticed window."

On the desk was the manuscript of Verne's last novel, *Sens Dessus, Dessous*. It told a fabulous story of Americans who, for the sake of speculation, made an attempt to change the axis of the earth so as to turn polar regions into fertile gardens. It told of sky writing and of Americans, seated in their own living rooms, receiving news bulletins from the planets Jupiter and Mars.

"A purely imaginary story," Jules Verne said wistfully. Nell touched the manuscript with awe. She noticed the neat French script, the many careful corrections made in the margins. Verne told her this was his tenth copy.

They passed from the study through an enormous library lined from ceiling to floor with books. In the hall, Verne pointed to a map tracing the course of his hero, Phineas Fogg, and marked on it the places where Nellie Bly's route would differ from it.

"If you do it in seventy-nine days," he told Nell, "I shall applaud with both hands. But seventy-five days—*mon Dieu* —that would be a miracle!"

Nell said farewell over a glass of wine and a French biscuit. *"Dieu vous garde!"* said Jules Verne, then added in English, clinking his glass to hers, "Good luck, Nellie Bly."

Mme. Verne kissed Nell on both cheeks, and she and her husband went out into the icy courtyard bareheaded to see Nell off. Nell's last sight of the famous Frenchman was of him waving after her carriage, his white hair flying in the wind. He seemed to her at that moment like the spirit Ariel in *The Tempest*, belonging far more to the realm of unlimited sky and space than to an earth of narrow concepts and endless frustrations.

But if his trips were fantasy, Nell's was reality. Off in the distance she heard the plaintive soprano of the European train whistle, so unlike the youthful blast of an American one. Her watch said she still had half an hour. But English and French trains, she was learning painfully, were weird and unpredictable. Could it be that the train for Calais this week was ahead of schedule?

"Hurry!" she called to the coachman, and when he did not understand her she broke into her very best French. He gave her a look of horror, whipped up his horses, and drove like mad. She had told him it was a matter of life or death and he had taken it to be a threat of his own execution.

The *World* had been waiting anxiously to hear from Nellie Bly. After her first cable, they had received fragmentary reports on her trip to Amiens from London and French papers. And then silence. They stalled while they reminded their readers that foreign trains were notoriously unreliable, and discussed the dangers that lay ahead of Nell on land and sea. But on November 24 they were able to announce to their now apprehensive audience that Nellie Bly had again been heard from. Not only had she visited the renowned Jules Verne, but she had made connections with the Brindisi mail train against fearful odds.

From Calais Nell had mailed back her Verne interview, and sent this cable message: "To all kind friends in America, good-by for the present. It took sharp work to catch the Brindisi mail train, but I got it."

Nell had dashed through England, across the Channel to Calais and Amiens, and back again to Calais, the *World* revealed, with just one hour to spare. She should be called "Nellie Fly" instead of "Nellie Bly," in their opinion. She would cross the Italian Alps now and, if nothing delayed her, should arrive at Brindisi on schedule, November 25. But there she must wait for a Pacific and Oriental steamer, and how long that wait would be no one knew.

Jules Verne was following her progress with elation, the Paris press reported. When the Russian government got around to completing the Trans-Siberian railroad, the trip could be made more easily. As it was now, Verne regarded her attempt as being an adventure as fabulous as any he had imagined.

"The whole civilized world is watching Nellie Bly," exclaimed the *World*. Rival New York papers agreed with the British that a mere woman could never be expected to beat the record of the remarkable Phineas Fogg, but the out-of-town American press was rooting for Nell's success. The Auburn, Maine, *Gazette* acclaimed Nell's trip "a journalistic daisy," and the Pennsylvania papers whooped it up for their native daughter in prose and verse. "She has no ordinary mind," proclaimed the Scranton *Sun*. "She is a pioneer of her sex."

More and more mail poured into the *World*. Songs and

THE WORLD.

NEW YORK, SUNDAY, JANUARY 26, 1890.

PAGES 21 TO 28.

ROUND THE WORLD WITH NELLIE BLY.

CUT OUT THIS GAME, PLACE IT ON A TABLE OR PASTE IT ON CARDBOARD AND PLAY ACCORDING TO SIMPLE DIRECTIONS BELOW.

(Copyrighted 1800.)

verses were being hastily composed in Nell's honor, some, the paper admitted, decidedly on the rocky side. A Nellie Bly game was invented. A ladies' dressing gown was to be named the "Nellie Bly wrapper."

And this was only the beginning of the Nellie Bly boom!

But Nellie Bly, seated in a private compartment of the Brindisi mail train with two strangers for companions, one a Frenchman, the other an Egyptian, knew nothing about all this. She felt cut off from the *World* and all that was happening at home. She had been stared at by one too many foreigners, and now, as she glanced out of the dirty window, she felt the strangers' eyes taking in her unchaperoned state with great boldness. Anything could happen in a compartment train, she thought, and shivered from cold, fatigue, and a sudden case of nerves. Then, because she was a reporter first, last, and always, she jotted down some notes:

"At Calais, I walked down to the empty pier at eleven-thirty at night and surveyed the revolving lighthouse, the most perfect of its kind in the world. As I watched the stars and moon shine down, I wondered if the natives of Calais ever bother to come out at night and see the miracle in their own town."

Nell glanced up and gave the bold strangers stare for stare now. Then she recorded:

"Small wonder the American girl is fearless. She does

not have to endure being shut up with strangers in a so-called private railway compartment. How much safer and more comfortable are the open coaches back home. There is safety in crowds. European girls *need* chaperones!"

When the train passed the customs at Modena, a guard entered the compartment and called, "Unlock your boxes." Nell showed him her one unlocked gripsack. He seemed skeptical at first that anyone, particularly a lady, could be traveling so unencumbered. Then, satisfied she was telling the truth, he laughed and told her not to bother opening such insignificant luggage.

Nell went gratefully to the sleeping section, where there were twenty-two passengers to keep her company. She was told that bandits had held up this train last week, and on this pleasant bedtime story climbed into her berth, piling all her clothing over her to keep from freezing.

Next morning she awoke early and pulled up the shade. She knew she was passing through Italy, but a heavy fog hid the landscape from her. She dressed and asked the train guard if this was usual Italian weather.

"It is a most extraordinary thing," he said. "I never saw a fog like this in Italy before."

Was this in her honor, Nell wondered. "All day I traveled through 'sunny Italy' along the Adriatic Sea," she wrote. "All day the fog continued. Then just at sunset we stopped at a station. The fog lifted. I saw a high rugged mountain, and near the foot a charming inn."

Nell entered with other passengers and was served a delicious dinner by a pretty Italian girl. The girl held out her hand for tips, but, when Nell gave one, to her bewilderment the proprietor father refused to let the girl accept it.

"Don't mind. Italians are the poorest and proudest people on earth," the train guard told Nell, "and they hate the English."

"But I am an American," said Nell. She turned back to compliment the Italian on his fine cooking and let him know her nationality.

"An American?" He had believed only Indians lived in America, he said. He permitted his daughter to take Nell's British coin now, but insisted on giving her a bottle of wine in exchange.

Nell boarded the train just as the starting horn blew and in spite of its snaillike progress it was only two hours late in reaching Brindisi.

Now was the supreme test, getting a ship for the Orient. When would one sail? Nell set her lips to keep them from trembling, twisted her ring. A miracle, Jules Verne had said. So let there be a miracle.

There was one. The Pacific and Oriental steamer *Victoria* was in port, waiting for passengers and ready to sail.

The relief was so great that tears came to Nell's eyes.

Such good fortune must be a sign to hasten her toward success. Her long lonely train trip had worn her down; it would be good to be with people again. But in this anticipation there were certain reservations, as she rode in an omnibus to the pier and followed her companions slowly up the gangplank.

"I rather feared meeting the many English people on this

boat, with their much talked-about prejudices," wrote Nell. "As it was now after one in the morning, I hoped everybody would be in bed."

But the crowd on deck dispelled Nell's hopes. She looked around for the purser and found none. Finally, with the aid of an unintroduced Englishman who had the courage to speak to her, the officer was located. She handed him a letter of introduction which explained she was traveling alone and should be given all the care and attention it was in his power to bestow. The purser read the letter with British aloofness, and then directed Nell to the wrong stateroom. Only after some effort was she relocated in her proper place. She found her cabin mate to be a New Zealand girl, full of fun and life.

Once settled, Nell asked the purser if she would have time to go to the cable office.

"If you hurry," he informed her indifferently. She realized she could miss the boat for all he cared.

As she started down the gangplank, she met the guard from her train, and he offered to show her where the cable office was. She followed him along dark narrow streets for what seemed to her miles. Finally they entered a dingy room lit by one smoky lamp. A sleepy-eyed Italian operator spoke to Nell in Queen Victoria's English:

"What can I do for you, Madam?"

"I want to send a cable to New York City."

"New York City?" he looked bewildered. "Where in thunder is it?"

Nell did not know whether to be amused or furious as she explained to the best of her ability where New York was. With the aid of books and documents, they figured out the cost of a cable to this "obscure place in faroff United States of America," which seemed the center of the universe to Nellie Bly. Precious time was consumed before she finally could dispatch her last European message to the *World*:

"November 25: I reached Brindisi this morning, after an uneventful trip across the continent. The railway journey was tedious and tiresome, but I received no end of courtesy from the railway officials. I found the steamship *Victoria* waiting, and in a few hours will be on the bosom of the Mediterranean. I am quite well, though somewhat fatigued. I send greetings to all friends in United States."

"Hurry, Madam," the train guard begged her. "We have no time left."

Nell threw down some money, clasped his hand, and together they made a mad dash through the streets. As they neared the pier they saw a steamer moving away. Nell nearly fainted, but the guard pulled her along. It was a steamer bound for India; the *Victoria* was still at the dock.

With less than five minutes to spare, Nell got on board. She knew herself now to be cut off from all contact with her beloved "upstart" country, the United States of America. The cable episode had convinced her of that. Here in this floating world completely dominated by English customs and ideals she was acutely aware how far away and unimportant America seemed to the rest of the globe, and how far-reaching and powerful Queen Victoria's Brittania was.

In spirit as well as fact it was no idle boast of the English in that year 1889 that the sun never set on the British Empire.

CHAPTER XVI

STRANDED—IN THE WORLD OF
QUEEN VICTORIA

BUT if Nell was cut off from the *World,* the *World* was also cut off from Nellie Bly. It was not until December 8 that her letter mailed from Southampton, England, could be published. The details of her visit to Jules Verne arrived many days later.

Meanwhile, the editors were left to imagine as best they could Nell's adventures and vicissitudes on the high seas. They had to report that another steamer, the *Germania,* had gone to a watery grave. They discussed monsoons, typhoons, and siroccos. They reminded *World* readers that, even though Nell had crossed Europe like a swallow and made extraordinary time because of good luck and her own fortitude, there were great obstacles ahead of her.

A national guessing contest was launched, with a round trip to Europe and fifty English pounds as the grand prize. Soon everybody in America seemed busy trying to figure out the exact time it would take Nellie Bly to circumnavigate the globe. Shopgirls, society women, suffragettes, businessmen, clergymen, senators and the ex-Governor of

A FREE TRIP TO EUROPE!

(Including first-class transatlantic passages, railroad fares and hotel bills)

TO THE PERSON WHO FIRST MAKES

THE NEAREST GUESS

AS TO THE

EXACT TIME OF NELLIE BLY'S TOUR.

NEXT SUNDAY'S WORLD

WILL PRINT A

NELLIE BLY BLANK BALLOT.

Upon this blank ballot all guesses must be made, the ballots being cut out and mailed to THE SUNDAY WORLD. Guesses not made on THE WORLD blanks cannot compete. Only one guess can be made on a single blank, but any reader of THE SUNDAY WORLD can send in as many guesses as he or she pleases, by procuring extra blanks from extra copies of THE SUNDAY WORLD. Full particulars Sunday. There will be an extraordinary demand for these blank ballots, and you should not fail to

Order Next SUNDAY'S WORLD at Once.

Louisiana were among the guessers. Many thought Nell would do well to come through in one hundred days, if she came through at all. Others claimed she could do it in eighty as Phineas Fogg did. A scattered few hoped for seventy-five.

An office staff was kept busy answering queries about Nellie Bly's life. Yes, she really was a girl, not a man, as many people insisted. She was a pretty brunette, the *World* revealed, quiet and reserved. She loved horseback riding and could ride a tricycle. She did not chew gum! Yes, there were other girl reporters in America but very few of them. No, Nellie Bly was not hiding out in New York as some claimed. She was actually on the high seas at this moment! Had she ever been in love? That, avowed the *World,* was something they would neither disclose nor discuss.

There was also much speculation about Nellie Bly aboard the steamship *Victoria.* Before the second day at sea, Nell discovered that the ship's gossipy purser had spread the rumor that she was a rich and eccentric American heiress, traveling unescorted around the world, carrying only a toothbrush and a bankbook. There were many males aboard, and Nell found herself much pursued. But some of her suitors were openly fortune hunters.

On a languid evening, as she lingered on deck listening to the passengers sing, "Who'll Buy My Silver Herring" an insistent gentleman took Nell's arm and guided her to a secluded nook. He began conversation by pointing out the mystery and beauty of the Mediterranean, and ended by asking Nell to marry him. When she hinted there might be some ulterior motive in his sudden courtship, he admitted with candor there was. He was a second son, he told her. His brother would get both money and family title. Therefore, he must find a wife quickly who would settle a thousand pounds a year on him.

"But I've grown to love you, too," he added.

Nell eyed him mischievously. "Would you love me as much if you found I am not a wealthy American heiress, but a poor girl being sent around the world for my health by a benevolent society?"

"Ah, my deah," he said, distressed, "that accounts for your inadequate wardrobe."

But her inadequate wardrobe brought her her most remarkable proposal, one from an impeccably groomed gentleman on board who had traveled since he was nine years old.

"I have always put down the desire to marry," he told Nell, in asking her to become his wife, "because I never expected to find a woman who could travel without innumerable trunks and bundles."

Since Nell had observed his faultless grooming and the fact that he changed three times a day, she asked him curiously:

"How many trunks do you have with you?"

"Nineteen."

She laughed.

"No wonder you need a wife with one gripsack!"

But most of Nell's companions on the *Victoria* were congenial and without ulterior motive. Her pretty New Zealand roommate had a brother on board and neither girl lacked for desirable escorts.

The chief unpleasantness Nell encountered was due to the ship's officials, whose pompous manners and air of superiority challenged her American spirit. They never ceased to remind her that the *Victoria*, like all things British, was the finest afloat, although Nell found the food of indifferent quality and indifferently served, cold soup and cold coffee being the rule. The cabins, too, were poorly planned, with many cut off completely from light and air.

On hot sultry nights many of the men passengers left their cabins and slept on deck, promenading in the early morning in their night clothes. The women, even Nell, lacked the courage to do this, although sometimes, when their cabin grew too stifling, Nell and her roommate slipped out and found a dark corner near the sailors' quarters where they listened long past midnight to the sounds of tom-toms and the weird chanting of the ship's crew. They fascinated Nell.

"The sailors on the *Victoria*," she wrote, "were Lascars. Most of them were untidy-looking. They wore brgiht turbans and went barefoot. They were a grim, surly set, climbing over the ship like a pack of monkeys, but we enjoyed their strange songs."

On the afternoon of November 27, exactly on Nell's schedule, the *Victoria* anchored at Port Said. It was Nell's first glimpse of the East. As the passengers went ashore, the men armed themselves with canes to keep off beggars, and the women carried parasols. Nell went empty-handed.

"A stick beats more ugliness into a person than out," she declared.

But the ship's officers were of different opinion. The *Victoria* was surrounded by a fleet of small boats, steered by half-clad Arabs, fighting, grabbing, punching, and yelling in mad haste to be first to earn a few pence for carrying passengers ashore. The captain ordered the sailors to fend them off with long poles. Nell marveled at the Arabs' stubborn persistence, even while cringing under blows.

Once ashore, Arab boys leading burros of all sizes surrounded Nell and her party. "Here's Gladstone," they shouted to the men. "Take a ride on him. See Gladstone with two beautiful black eyes." They called out to the ladies, "This burro is Mary Anderson. Ride a stage beauty. Ride Lily Langtry!"

Every little animal was named for a British favorite. Nell, who had ridden burros in Mexico, mounted one and went gaily trotting through the streets of the quaint town. When the sightseeing was finished the passengers all went into a gambling house where an orchestra composed entirely of young women was playing, a sight Nell had never seen before, even in advanced America.

The passengers returned to the ship as darkness fell, walking past houses with elaborately carved wooden fronts. Nell learned with astonishment that it was in these the very poor lived. But everyone seemed very poor here. Though the Egyptian women were heavily veiled, the children they carried were naked. Beggars were on every hand, showing deformities and pleading for alms. Nell dodged a mangy camel carrying firewood and did not need the urging of the guide to hurry along. The boatmen at the wharf warned the sightseers that the *Victoria* might sail without them, then demanded double pay because it was past sunset.

Next morning, Nell rose early to see the famous Suez Canal. She was disappointed in that too.

"It was an enormous ditch," she wrote, "enclosed on either side with high sandbanks. The speed limit was five knots an hour because a rapid passage of ships would make a strong current and wash in the sandbanks." She was told that the canal, completed twenty years before in 1869, had cost the lives of a hundred thousand laborers.

The trip through took twenty-four hours. About noon of the first day in the canal the *Victoria* anchored in the bay, fronting Ismailia, to take on passengers. As the steamer resumed its slow journey, naked Arabs ran along the banks crying, "Baksheesh—baksheesh," while passengers flung coins to them. They dropped anchor again in the Bay of Suez where Nell was told the Israelites crossed the Red Sea. The ship was surrounded by sailboats carrying fruits, odd shells, and souvenirs. A black juggler came aboard, wearing a turban and little else but a sash. Eyeing the passengers, he selected Nell from the crowd to hold his large handkerchief while he did a trick.

"He showed us a small brass bangle and pretended to put it in his handkerchief," wrote Nell. "Then he placed the handkerchief in my hand, telling me to hold it tightly. I did so, feeling the presence of the bangle very plainly. He blew on it, and jerking the handkerchief loose from my grasp, shook it. Much to the amazement of the crowd, the bangle was gone."

After he left, taking the passengers' coins with him, Nell was asked if she knew how the trick was done. She explained it was a very old and simple trick. He merely had one bangle sewed in his handkerchief.

"Why didn't you expose him?" demanded an Englishman.

Nell grinned. "I wanted to see the poor fellow get his money," she said, much to the gentleman's disgust.

The next morning the *Victoria* was on the Red Sea, well out of sight of land. The weather was very hot, and the young men put on a minstrel show and served punch and biscuits to the passengers. Nell wore her light silk bodice and was sure no one was more comfortable than she was.

It was a gay and pleasant interlude. Eager as she was to make time, there was nothing Nell could do on the boat to speed her own progress. Once she had completed her stories for the day she could relax and enjoy herself, and she did. But sometimes in the evenings she would slip away from her companions, however congenial, and find a deserted corner of the deck and sit quietly watching the moonlight on the water, and the realization would come to her, "Much as I like excitement and adventure and people, I like best of all to be alone."

She recalled with an ironic little smile that she had first

thought of the trip because she wanted to get away to the ends of the earth. But there were people there too, she'd found. Friendly people, most of them. She was grateful for them. But always there was so much pressure. Wistfully she admitted she never seemed to have time any more to be herself, to be Elizabeth Cochrane. Pinky had been swallowed up in Nellie Bly.

But, when they dropped anchor at Aden, she was gayest of the gay. The passengers were warned not to leave the ship because of the intense heat. But Nell with a few other reckless ones went ashore. They hired a carriage and drove along wide smooth roads past adobe huts, beggars, tribesmen of every nation, a camel market, and a goat market to the English fort.

"No matter where I went," observed Nell, "I saw English soldiers stationed, and as I traveled on, I realized more than ever how the English have all the desirable seaports. I cease to marvel at the pride with which the Englishmen view their flag floating in so many climes over so many different nations."

It made her thoughtful. Hourly now she was reminded of the importance and majesty of Queen Victoria's empire. Everywhere, English money was acceptable, while American money—gold, silver, and paper—was held in contempt. On shipboard, Nell heard the nightly singing of "God Save the Queen," and, whenever Queen Victoria's picture was shown during a lantern-slide program, tremendous applause showed the loyalty and high esteem in which her countrymen held her.

Nell was made especially aware of her lone status as an American when, one evening shortly after the ship left Aden for Colombo, Ceylon, the young ladies aboard decided to put on a *tableau vivant* representing the different countries. Wanting Nell to represent America, they asked her to tell them what the American flag looked like so they could make one as a drape. Nell could scarcely keep back tears as she described it to them, for it suddenly came over her that *she had not seen the American flag once since leaving home!*

The *Victoria* anchored at Colombo next morning. Nellie Bly in her homesick mood discovered with consternation that, before the China-bound steamer *Oriental* could leave the harbor, it must wait for the ancient *Nepal* to come in. And that might easily be ten days.

In America, the Nellie Bly Guessing Match was gaining momentum everywhere. Out-of-town newspaper dealers reported that they could not get enough copies of the New York *World*. The Rochester *Post Express*, already anticipating Nell's arrival home, reported blizzards in some parts of the nation and declared: "The American blizzard should be patriotic enough to get off the track when Nellie Bly starts on her tour across the continent, but the bliz cannot always be depended on."

December 10, the day Nell was scheduled to arrive at Ceylon, came and went, but where was the Nellie Bly? The *World* was really worried. Either the cable service in the

Orient was worse than feared, or Nell had been shanghaied, lost at sea, or who knew what? But on December 14 the *World,* after trying to locate her, reassured its waiting public: "No message has been received from Nellie Bly, but very probably she has sailed from Ceylon."

They kept up their own spirits and those of their readers by improvising tales of what Nell had probably seen while on the Isle of Ceylon and would find in Singapore. "Did she see the Buddha's tooth and collarbone?" asked the *World.* "Will she visit the gorgeous Buddhist temples? She may ride in a native catamaran, go berrying in coffee fields, or join in an elephant hunt. She may rock in a howdah on the back of a giant pachyderm!"

But, in the midst of the descriptions of oriental splendor, they instructed their busy guessers at home and abroad to guess early and often, for "Nell still has at least 13,500 miles to go." The favorite guessing time, they added, was seventy-nine or eighty days.

But the New York *Metropolis* struck a sour note: "She may be shipwrecked or fall ill from some tropical disease or the trains may be delayed. There is no possible basis for calculating Nellie Bly's time."

"Colombo is a pleasant place to stay," Nell was told comfortingly when she received the disheartening information that she would have an indefinite wait on the Island of Ceylon.

"It might be," she said dismally, "if getting away from here did not mean more than life to me."

But she checked in at the Grand Oriental Hotel, run by a titled German. She freshened up, ate a delicious meal of shrimps and boiled rice, chicken, beef and preserved fruits served by immaculate Singhalese waiters who spoke English fluently, and her spirits revived.

Some pleasant acquaintances she had made on shipboard came to her rescue: a Spanish consul, a jolly Irish lad, the New Zealand girl and her brother. And soon she was on friendly terms with the Englishman who ran Ceylon's one newspaper, and who gave Nell quite a whirl. All of these people now knew the object of her journey around the world, and did their best to cheer her up. Since no one could predict for certain when the *Oriental* would sail, Nell deferred further reports to her paper until she had more facts to go on. Meanwhile, she found Colombo as pleasant a place to be as was possible under the nerve-racking circumstances.

There was a blue harbor with a high mountain, Adam's Peak, in the background; a forest of tropical trees lined the beach. During the day everybody lounged around the hotel grounds. The men smoked, consumed gallons of whisky and soda, and perused old newspapers; the women sipped cool lime drinks, read novels, or bargained, Nell reported. Dresses were cheaper than in America. Nell bought a summer gown, "better than Worth's," for five rupees, about two and a half dollars.

"For the first time since leaving America, I saw American money," recorded Nell. "It is very popular in Colombo and commands a high price—as jewelry! The Colombo diamond merchants are glad to get American twenty-dollar gold pieces, and pay a premium for them. They put a ring through them and hang them on their watch chains for ornaments. The richer the merchant, the more American gold dangles from his chain. But when I offered it in payment for my bills, I was told it would be taken at 60 per cent discount."

After dinner it was the custom to go driving or bicycle riding. Colombo reminded Nell of Newport, Rhode Island; its smooth roads, laid by convicts, were the finest she had ever seen. With her escort, she went by moonlight in a bullock hackery to the Parsee theater where all the parts were played by men actors. She rode in her first jinricksha to see the temples of Colombo, and met the famous high priest of Ceylon, who told Nell he had converts in faroff America. She went too to a Kandy, but the Buddha's tooth and collarbone in the musty old temple there did not impress her half so much as Peradeniya's beautiful botanical gardens.

On her way home from Kandy, the heat and strain from waiting around for four days gave Nell a violent headache. Since cholera was prevalent on the island, her friends feared she might be coming down with it. But her symptoms disappeared when she received word that the following morning the *Oriental* would sail for China.

She felt tired and nervous, however, as she hurried aboard the ship at five o'clock. She found the ship practically deserted, except for the chief engineer and the ship's doctor, a young Welshman named Brown.

She said anxiously, "I thought the *Nepal* was here."

"She was to have been at daybreak," Nell was told. "She's delayed again. She is a slow old boat."

Nell's face flushed. She saw herself forlornly creeping back to New York ten days behind time, afraid to hear her name spoken. For the first time she lost her temper.

"I hope she goes to the bottom of the sea when she does get in," she said angrily. "I think *it is an outrage* to be held up for a tub like that."

Dr. Brown looked at Nell's burning cheeks with concern. He too seemed to suspect she was ill.

"I'm all right, Doctor," said Nell with a shamefaced grin. "The only thing the matter with me is that I must win this race against Time."

He looked at her sympathetically.

"We'll help you all we can," he told her. But she knew he was powerless.

It was noon when the old "tub" *Nepal* hove in sight. The *Oriental* sailed out of the blue Ceylon bay at 1:00 P.M. Nell had cabled the *World*: "Detained at Colombo for five days." Now she breathed a deep sigh and sniffed the rose-sweet sea air.

The *Oriental* was a smaller ship than the *Victoria,* but a nicer one, in Nell's opinion. The cabins were light and airy, and the ship's officials, from Captain down, polite but not stuffy. The weather was perfect, and days and nights passed like a languid dream. Almost before Nell knew it, the ship had anchored off the beautiful green island of Penang, or Prince of Wales Island. There, with a six-hour stopover,

Nell and Dr. Brown went ashore on a sampan, an oddly shaped boat, with Malay oarsmen. Then visited a Chinese joss house adorned with dragons, exotic lanterns, and gilt ornaments. They saw a Hindu temple, but Nell refused to remove her shoes, so she could not enter.

The Malays were a proud race, Nell learned, too proud to speak English. Mexican silver was used almost exclusively in Penang. American silver had some value, but American gold was refused. American paper money was laughed at.

The ship moved on to rough water, and the pirate-infested strait of Penang, but the *Oriental* reached Singapore two days later. Nell was beginning to feel hopeful that she could make up lost time when she was told they must anchor outside the harbor until morning as it was too dangerous to make port after dark. This delay meant that the *Oriental* could not leave Singapore for Hong Kong until the following night.

"I was in an agony of suspense," Nell wrote. "A single hour lost now meant much to me. I felt I was wasting precious time lying just outside the gate of hope; this might mean missing my ship at Hong Kong."

But there was nothing she could do about it. So, controlling her impatience, the next morning she and the young doctor went ashore to see the sights of Singapore.

They hired a ricksha and Nell got her first glimpse of Chinese streets without sidewalks. They were narrow and crowded and filthy. The dirt and general squalor contrasted oddly with enormously long brightly tinted fingernails displayed by the most ragged beggar. There were other incongruities. At the cable office where she sent a code message to the *World*, English was spoken and American silver was accepted at par. But her gold and paper money were worthless here.

Nell and Dr. Brown had dinner at the Hotel de L'Europe. As they rode away, their Malay driver pulled the gharry to one side for a funeral procession. They heard a blast of trumpets, and musicians on Malay ponies came past, making strange discordant noises on fifes and cymbals. Men followed on foot carrying roast pigs on long poles and bearing Chinese lanterns. In the rear were about forty pallbearers. The casket was carried on poles and covered with a scarlet cloth. It was a strange and startling sight to these occidentals.

Nell found that no foreigners were permitted in the Mohammedan temples, and that women were not permitted in the Chinese Hindu temples, even when they removed their shoes. When a sacred cow fastened by a pin to the grass outside a Hindu temple looked at Nell menacingly, she decided to get away fast. She was told that if a sacred cow went after a foreigner, the Chinese considered it their duty to let the beast kill the infidel.

On her way back to the ship, a small Singapore monkey looked at Nell from a cage, its eyes pleading. Nell could not resist the eager, almost human little face. She bought it. It became a source of both amusement and trouble for the rest of her journey.

The *Oriental* sailed for Hong Kong at night and ran

directly into a monsoon. Nell found it a beautiful though terrifying thing to watch. But as the sea swelled and head winds tore at the ship, most of the passengers became seasick and fearful.

The Irish lad, for whom Nell had developed a great fondness, stretched out in a willow chair with a bottle of champagne at his elbow, and declared that, if they ever reached Hong Kong, he would stay there forever unless he could return to England overland. His English roommate, he said, had gone to bed every night with a life preserver on, and had bailed out the cabin with a cigarette box.

His roommate put in, "While I was bailing out the cabin, this boy clung to the upper berth groaning and praying."

"One bride on this trip," wrote Nell, "has not taken off her life preserver since she left home."

On a particularly rough night, one suitor of Nell's staggered after her to the heaving deck. The water washed over them in a foaming crest, and, as the pair clung to the railing, he invited Nell to jump overboard with him. "Death by drowning," he assured her, "is a peaceful slumber and a quiet drifting away."

Nell declined. Life was still sweet to her. But as she made her way back to the cabin, it seemed almost certain that the end was near for both ship and passengers. Her cabin floor was covered with water. As she crawled into her bunk, the magnitude of the monsoon made her personal worries seem trivial. It appeared she might not get around the world in a hundred days, or ever.

"But at this point I believed in letting unchangeable things go," she wrote. "If the ship was going down there was time enough to worry when it went. With that conclusion I fell asleep."

Her courage was rewarded and in spite of the monsoon the *Oriental* arrived in Hong Kong two days ahead of schedule.

On December 22, those of the passengers who were in any condition to do so, Nell among them, sang Christmas carols and said their farewells. A cannon was fired as the ship entered port, and Portuguese lorchas, Chinese junks and sampans bobbed up and down in the dirty water. Nell and several companions left the boat together and were carried in sedan chairs through the crowded streets.

"My one desire was to get as speedily as possible to the office of the Oriental and Occidental Steamship Company," wrote Nell, "to learn the earliest date I could leave for Japan to continue my race around the world. I was particularly elated because the good ship *Oriental* had not only made up for the five days I had lost in Colombo but had reached Hong Kong two days before it was due, and that with the terrible northeast monsoon against her. It was the *Oriental's* maiden trip to China, this one from Colombo to Hong Kong, *and I had had the good fortune to be on her when she broke all previous records!*"

It was quite a thrill.

But Nell's feeling of elation changed quickly when she reached the steamship office.

"You will have to lay over five days here and five more in Yokohama," a swarthy agent told her, eyeing her furtively. "But that won't matter to you now. You are out of the race anyhow, Miss Bly. The *World* sent out another reporter the day you left."

"*Another reporter?*" Nell stared at the man in utter bewilderment. "A man? A woman?"

"A woman. She was to race you," the agent explained "She is now well ahead of you and you can't catch up. She has already left Hong Kong."

"What is her name?" Nell demanded.

"I am not permitted to give you that information. But I assure you it is true. So you may as well forget the whole business."

"I can't believe this. Have you any cables or messages for me from New York?" Nell asked desperately.

"Nothing," the man told her and turned away.

As Nell stood in near panic, the purser of the *Oceanic,* the ship on which Nell was scheduled to travel to Japan and then on to America, hurried up.

"Miss Bly?" he hailed her. "I am Mr. Fuhrman. I'm certainly relieved to find you. I went down to the *Oriental* to meet you and you had left. I thought you were lost."

"I *am* lost," said Nell and poured out her troubles.

"It is a fantastic affair, and a contemptible trick if the *World* did it," Mr. Furhman told her when she had finished. "But you should not feel too badly. You have had the worst possible weather. And everybody knows the idea of such a trip originated with you."

188

"I promised my paper I would make the trip in seventy-five days," said Nellie slowly. "If I accomplish that I am satisfied. I did not agree to race against any one or anything but Time. Still—*to send someone else—and not tell me. . . .*"

She said nothing more, but her heart was broken.

CHAPTER XVII

WE'LL WIN OR DIE

ONCE again, on opposite sides of the earth, the *World* and Nellie Bly alike were troubled and disturbed. New York had heard of the raging monsoons that were sweeping the eastern seas. And the cablegrams they were receiving signed "Nellie Bly," didn't seem to add up. They had believed through the code there could be no confusion, but it appeared the *World* was getting false reports.

On December 19 the *World* announced in headlines, NELLIE BLY REACHED SINGAPORE YESTERDAY. But it admitted that conflicting messages had come into the office and that the staff was puzzled.

"Though the unswerving luck of this plucky Nell will no doubt prevail against the dreadful monsoons and typhoons, the public is cautioned not to be overly optimistic. Last Monday we received from Nellie Bly in Colombo this cable: 'Detained here for five days.' But another cable announced her arrival in Singapore and a third said she reached Hong

Kong two days ahead of schedule. Did she send the wrong cable from Colombo? How did she get from Ceylon to China in five days? Did the Mahatmas help her? Did she project her astral body through space?"

The public's guess was as good as the *World's*. On December 25, having had no further word from her and with wild rumors flying, the office sent a cablegram to her in care of the American consul at Hong Kong wishing her a Merry Christmas and a Happy New Year. The newspaper speculated in print how Nell would spend the holiday if she was in this faraway Chinese city. The weather would be hot, said the *World*; however, there would be curious sights and strange and interesting people.

"Will Nellie Bly be amazed to meet the American dollar in the midst of ancient methods, men and machinery?" the *World* asked, and added nostalgically, "Will she miss the holly wreath and red berries back home?"

At approximately that hour Nellie Bly was crying. It was Christmas day and she was far from home and holly berries. But there, waving over the gateway of the American Consulate in Canton, she saw the Stars and Stripes for the first time since she had left New York. She burst into happy tears. It was a wonderful Christmas present.

After transferring her baggage and pet monkey from the *Oriental* to the *Oceanic*, Nell and a group of friends had started from Hong Kong by Chinese steamer on Christmas Eve. She had seen nothing but squalor and misery in Hong Kong and was finding more of it in Canton. But this moment was one of happiness and pride. As Nell watched her national banner floating in the breeze, she took off her peaked cap and stood at salute.

"That is the most beautiful sight in the world and I am ready to whip anyone who says it isn't," she declared solemnly.

Nell's English friends looked at her flag with new respect and no one said a word.

Consul Seymour gave Nell and her party a warm welcome and some serious warnings. They were not to be surprised if in Canton men threw stones at them and Chinese women spit in the faces of the women tourists. His dire predictions were not fulfilled, Nell wrote. The Chinese appeared to her to have seen nothing but trouble. Their one interest in her seemed to be in her gloves, which they touched gently as she passed by them.

There were many interesting things in Canton, fine shops and more than eight hundred temples, including the Temple of the Five Hundred Gods. There was also the Temple of Horrors. Its filthy stone steps were crowded with peddlers, lepers, cripples of every description, fortunetellers, and gamblers. Inside, figures representing the punishments in Buddhist hell were more gruesome than any Nell had seen. They showed caricatures of people being whipped, ground to death, boiled in oil, beheaded, and sawed in half.

Nell went through the leper village, which she termed "ghastly in misery," and visited the execution grounds, which looked like a crooked back alley in a country village. She saw many crosses there and the guide said coolly, "When women are condemned to death in China, they are bound to wooden crosses and then cut to pieces. Men are beheaded with one stroke unless they are the worst criminals; then they are given the death of a woman." Even here, she observed, in death as well as life, the men were the privileged sex. She began to understand the melancholy look on the faces of the Chinese people. They seemed to have no hope.

At the Canton jail, she saw other examples of Chinese torture. The prisoners wore thick heavy boards around their necks. She was shown a room filled with instruments of punishment, whips of split bamboo, thumb screws, pulleys on which people were suspended by their thumbs. In the courtroom the judges smoked opium and played fan-tan. Two men were brought in for stealing while she was there. They were chained with their knees meeting their chins, and carried in baskets suspended on a pole between two coolies. The judges left off smoking opium to pronounce sentence: every bone in the prisoners' hands was to be crushed under heavy stones. But afterwards Nell was assured, they would be sent to the hospital to be cured.

After having Christmas lunch in the Temple of the Dead, where hundreds of bodies had lain in caskets for seventy-five years or more, Nell was more than ready to return to the American Embassy. It was like a little oasis of comfort and cheer in a desert of agony. She was showered with presents and messages from European friends, and she and her party returned to Hong Kong, for foreigners were not permitted to stay in Canton after nightfall.

It had been a strange Christmas.

THE WORLD: SUNDAY, DECEMBER 29, 1889.

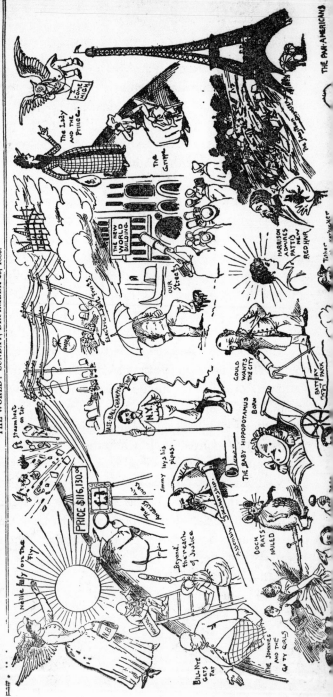

THE PAN-AMERICANS

COME HIGH.

The Lady and the Prince.

The Grippe.

HARRISON ADMIRES PATTI'S NEW RED HAIR.

THE NEW WORLD BUILDING.

OUR Streets.

ELECTRIC LIGHT TRUSTS.

GOULD WANTS THE CITY.

BATTERY PARK.

BASE-BALL CHAMPION.

N.Y.

Jimmy lays his pipes.

THE BABY HIPPOPOTAMUS BORN.

DOCK RATS NAILED.

ASSEMBLY STEAMSHIP.

Beyond the reach of Justice.

PRICE $116,130.00

Steam heat on tap.

BILL NYE GETS FAT.

THE JOHNNIES AND THE GAYETY GIRLS.

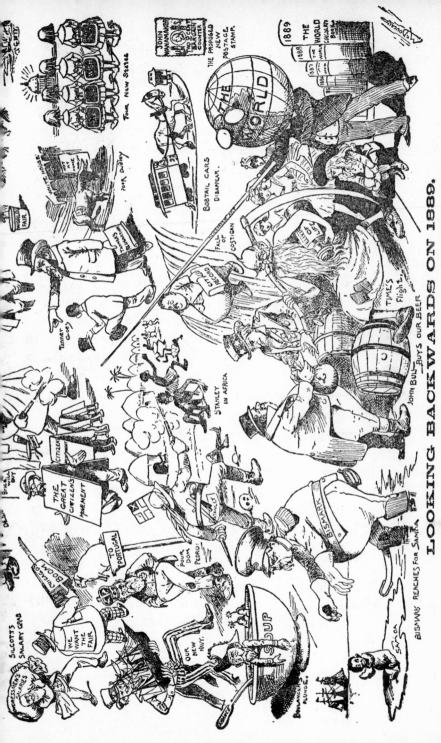

LOOKING BACKWARDS ON 1889.

Courtesy of The New York Public Library, New York City

On December 28, Nell, still upset by the rumor about the rival reporter but determined to do her best, set sail on the steamer *Oceanic* for Japan. Despite rough seas and bad winds, it made good time. On New Year's Eve, a little group of Anglo-Americans sat up to see in the New Year. "The year 1889 was ushered out forever," wrote Nell, "and the year 1890, with its pleasures and pain, welcomed in with 'Auld Lang Syne.'" On January 3, 1890, the ship arrived in the fairyland of Japan.

In Tokyo Nell saw the Mikado's palace and the famous Shiba Temple. Here she found a happy blending of European and Oriental culture. The men copied the more practical European styles, while the women continued to wear their delightful kimonos with flowers decorating their sweetly scented hair. There were superb streets in Tokyo, and on them bicycles and streetcars. The Japanese had retained the best features of their own culture and added the best features of Western civilization, Nell felt. They had permitted the Europeans to aid them, but retained control of their own government. Nell could not get over their progressiveness. Even the blind here seemed contented and hopeful, for the Japanese had set aside the massaging trade exclusively for this group and they did not have to resort to begging, as in so many countries.

"There is no greater mistake than to think the Chinese and Japanese are alike," Nell wrote. "Japan is a land of beauty, love, poetry, and cleanliness. The Japanese are a cheerful, happy people. Their food is excellent, and their dainty houses clean and doll-like."

In Yokohama, Nell was met by a dapper-looking Japanese newspaperman, who showed her a copy of the New York *World* with her Jules Verne interview. To her relief there was no mention in the *World* of any rival reporter. The Verne interview had been translated into Japanese, and she learned for the first time here of the stir her trip was creating at home, and of the Nellie Bly guessing contest, which seemed to be attracting the attention of the Japanese, as well as of all America.

She rode in a ricksha, pulled by a short-legged Jap in bright blue pants, to the office of the Oriental and Occidental Steamship Company. In the immaculate streets women in silk kimonos and children with happy faces played shuttlecock or flew kites. "Everything about Yokohama had a Sunday freshness," said Nell. "No one can imagine women and children playing shuttlecock or flying kites in the streets of Hong Kong."

Nell wired to her paper: "Yokohama, January 3: I arrived here safely and in good health after a six days' passage from Hong Kong, which we left on December 28. Quicker time could have been made between Hong Kong and this port, but an earlier arrival would have been of no avail, as the steamship *Oceanic* is advertised all through Japan to leave here on January 7, and mails will not be ready until that date. The commander of the *Oceanic* expects to make extra effort between here and San Francisco and may arrive there January 20. I hope to be in New York January 25. Happy New Year to all my friends in America."

Then Nell set out on another round of sightseeing, and

spent the three happiest days of her world-trotting expedition, visiting in Japanese homes and watching the fascinating geisha girls in their graceful dances. These doll-like little maidens took Nell to their hearts, exclaiming over her fashionable gown, gloves, bracelet, ring, and pretty hair. "They thought I was sweet," Nell wrote, "and I thought they were."

As she left this Eden on January 7, the ship's band played "Hail Columbia," "Home Sweet Home," and "The Girl I Left Behind Me." There was high excitement on board the *Oceanic*. Chief Engineer Allen had written and placed over the engine:

> For Nellie Bly
> We'll win or die!

"Everything went marvelously until the third day out," wrote Nell. "The *Oceanic* was 110 miles ahead of its last mark. Then came terrible storms. The next day was dreadful with head winds, high rolling, and pitching. In spite of the best efforts of the crew, the ship could make little progress."

The sailors all blamed the weather trouble on the Singapore monkey.

"Monkeys are Jonahs. Your pet is a jinx. Throw the animal overboard," they told Nell. "We'll make it then."

But jinx or no jinx, Nell refused to part with her pet. Failure seemed inevitable.

"If I fail," Nell told the chief engineer, "I will never return to New York. I have reached the point now where I would rather go in dead and successful than alive and a failure."

"I swore at this storm until I had no words left," Engineer Allen told her. "Then I prayed, and I haven't prayed in years."

"I've prayed too," Nell confessed. "I prayed, 'God be merciful to me, a sinner.' But the storm keeps right on. Can it be that I am not a sinner?"

The light words covered her longing and her dedication and her challenge of defeat. Through gales and heavy seas the *Oceanic* plowed on.

CHAPTER XVIII

SHE'S BROKEN EVERY RECORD

AMERICA too was having weather troubles. And the *World*, having backed Nell as she triumphed over bad communications, slow trains, delayed boats, monsoons, and Oriental diseases, now turned its attention to blizzard worries.

On January 4 the paper proudly published Nell's cable from Yokohama and the boom for Nell reached a new high. Nellie Bly guessing games were now the rage everywhere. Song and verse writers had a field day. Joe Hart, the popular comedian, threw together a composition called "Globe Trotting Nellie Bly" which he dedicated to the New York *World*. It was dreadful verse but the public loved it. It began:

> I hold here in my hand
> A lengthy telegram
> That comes from far across the sea.
> It's from Miss Nellie Bly
> And its message I will try
> To tell if you'll listen unto me.
> She's trying very hard
> To break the world's record
> To round the world in seventy-five days. . . .

Globe Trotting Nellie Bly.

Respectfully dedicated to the NEW YORK WORLD, by the popular comedians, HALLEN and HART.

Words and Music by Mr. JOE HART.

Allegro.

1. I hold here in my hand a lengthy ca - ble - gram, That came from far a - cross the sea............ Its from Miss Nel - lie Bly, and its con - tents I will try To tell, if you will lis - ten un - to me............ She's try - ing ve - ry hard to beat the world's re - cord To round the World in sev - en - ty - five Days........

It went on interminably. Others were shorter if not any more poetical. This was from Kinderhook *Rough Notes*:

> Nellie Bly
> Keeps her eye
> Wide open when she sleeps,
> And in the morning when she wakes
> She jots down heaps and heaps.

The Florida *Times Union* published this:

> Nellie Bly, Nellie Bly,
> You've surely got the drop
> Sent by the *World* around the world
> You spin it like a top.

There was real assurance of success in the one which ran:

> "Oh Fogg, good-by," said Nellie Bly.
> "It takes a maiden to be spry,
> To span the space 'twixt thought and act
> And turn a fiction to a fact."

And the *World* itself gave space to this rocky rhyme:

> To circumnavigate the globe
> Is a daring feat indeed,
> But you've been round the *World* so much
> I'm sure you will succeed.

The *World* and the world certainly hoped she would. Press clubs and citizens all across America—in San Francisco, Chicago, Omaha, Salt Lake City, Philadelphia, and Pittsburg—were preparing to give Nell a welcome when her train passed through. Then on January 15, with Nell now sixty-three days away from home, wild storms were reported on both coasts, with many shipwrecks. The entire country was swept by a new series of blizzards. Great herds of cattle perished on the Western plains. Trains sat for days in deep drifts. And in the Pacific the *Oceanic* tossed wildly.

Nell was so near yet so far away that all she had hoped for seemed about to be lost. The storm did not abate, the sea continued to run high, the waves were like mountains. Nature would give no help, and man could give none. Thousands waited in anguished suspense to learn the fate of the steamer on which depended not only Nellie Bly's success but her life.

And finally, pledged to win or to die, Nell won. Battered but triumphant, the *Oceanic* steamed into San Francisco Bay and word was flashed that Nellie Bly was back in her own country.

She was not, however. There was a further complication, Either by accident or intent, someone had started a rumor that there was smallpox on board the *Oceanic*. It was not true. But the ship's purser discovered he had left the ship's bill of health behind in Yokohama.

"What does that mean?" demanded the frantic Nell.

"It means we will have to wait in harbor until the next boat arrives from Japan."

"How long will that be?"

"About two weeks."

Two weeks. It might as well be a lifetime.

"I'll jump overboard and swim ashore," Nell announced firmly.

No one doubted she spoke the truth. Technicalities were dispensed with and Nell, with her gripsack and her monkey, was placed on a tugboat. She stuck out her tongue for, and probably at, the quarantine doctor, and the tug puffed away from the *Oceanic* toward the San Francisco shore.

Never in her rosiest dreams had Nellie pictured such an ovation as awaited her setting foot on American soil again. San Franciscans had been busy for days preparing her welcome. On hand to greet her were the Mayor, the San Francisco Press Club, suffragette groups, and most of the populace. She was showered with speeches of praise, songs, flowers, fruit. She was applauded and cheered while the band played "Nellie Blue Eyes" and "The Girl I Left Behind Me."

Nell faced them all, radiant, sun-browned, and triumphant.

"There's no place like home," she said. "For sixty-eight days I have been flying around the world and am once more back in America. The saddest sounds were the farewells called from the Hoboken pier. The sweetest, the word of welcome and applause in San Francisco."

But it was still too early for complete jubilation. Nell was whisked to the station of the Atlantic and Pacific Railroad, there to board a special train and begin the last lap of her race against Time.

No president had ever been acclaimed as homecoming

Nellie Bly was on her thrilling ride East. At every whistle stop, every hamlet, village, and city, the American people were waiting to applaud this girl who was making a dream come true. The only methods of communication were scattered telegraph facilities and a few telephones, all with wires disrupted by the storms. But news of Nell's approach spread like prairie fire. As her train rumbled by, people stood along the tracks to wave at her, greet her.

But, if it was a triumphant ride, it was a hazardous one too. Tracks were obstructed by snow-blinded or dead cattle; detours had to be made to avoid new blizzards. There were two near disasters the first days out. Once the train was almost derailed when it crashed into a handcar left on the tracks. The flying splinters showered Nellie and the newsmen on the platform with bits of steel and jagged splinters of wood. The second crisis came three miles east of Gallup, New Mexico, where track repairmen were repairing bridge stringers over a ravine a hundred feet deep. These were held in place only by jackscrews when the special bore down on the bridge. With no time to give warning, the workmen watched in horror as the bridge bent under the weight of the locomotive. But the jackscrews held!

Through New Mexico, Arizona, and Colorado Nell whizzed, relieving her eagerness for speed from time to time by taking the throttle and racing the engine at the unbelievable speed of sixty miles an hour. Indians signaled from their ponies as the train roared past; ranchers and their families came miles to get a glimpse of her. There were crowds at every station. As Nell waved from a rear platform, Kansas suffragettes shouted at her to come back and run for governor.

The excitement of the trip stimulated Nell's Singapore monkey. When Nell was trying to dictate stories of her adventures to a secretary, the monkey scampered from car to car, leading his mistress a merry chase. If the train stopped, he made it clear he considered himself and not Nell the reason for the show of interest.

In Chicago, members of the Chicago Press Club whisked Nell off for a breakfast reception between trains. There she was handed a message from Jules Verne, brimming with good wishes. Verne had reason to feel pleased. Nellie Bly was bringing him luck, as she had brought luck and happiness to so many others. His book, *Around the World in Eighty Days,* had gone into its tenth printing since Nell started her trip around the world. Now it was to be revived as a play at the Chatelet Theater in Paris, with Nell written into the epilogue, if she could beat the record of Phineas Fogg.

As Nell's train passed through Pittsburgh, the city seemed to her unchanged except for the final *h* in the name. With tear-filled eyes she stood on the rear platform, waving to her old newspaper crowd who had flocked to the station en masse to wish her Godspeed. One face only was missing from that gathering, the face of her dear Erasmus Wilson. He had not come to greet her, and it was then Nell understood that even moments of great wonder can have their heartache too.

But her disappointment gave way to new happiness when in Philadelphia Jules Chambers and Ballard Smith of the *World* and James Metcalfe, her man with the violet eyes, who since that first snowy encounter had become a close friend, boarded her special.

With them was Nell's mother, in a black velvet wrap and bonnet, beaming with pride.

"Nell isn't much of a girl for talking," she had told the waiting reporters. "I seldom know what she's about until I read it in the papers. I'm certainly glad she's so near home. Nell is the apple of my eye. She is all the world to me."

Now Nell flung her arms about the happy little lady. But over the velvet-clad shoulder she smiled at James Metcalfe as she called out excitedly, "I really think I'll make it now!"

And soon Nell's train pulled into Jersey City, where her round-the-world trip was to be timed.

The station was packed as the cars lurched to a stop, the people beside themselves with excitement. Police tried to push back the mob, but they pressed forward eagerly for a glimpse of America's first daughter. She jumped down on the grimy planking, waving her ghillie cap, her eyes shining. Three stop watches recorded the historic moment: 3:51 P.M.

"She's a winner! She's a winner!" the timekeepers shouted hoarsely. "Time: *Seventy-two days, six hours, ten minutes and eleven seconds!*"

"She's broken every record!" roared the people. "*She's a winner!*"

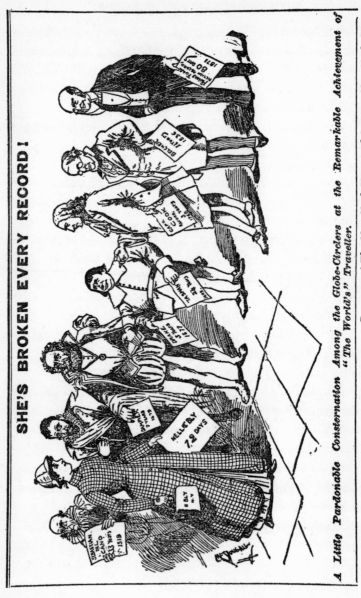

SHE'S BROKEN EVERY RECORD!

A Little Pardonable Consternation Among the Globe-Circlers at the Remarkable Achievement of "The World's" Traveller.

Courtesy of The New York Historical Society, New York City.

Now there was no holding them back. They surged forward, eager to touch this miracle girl, Nellie Bly, who had circled the globe not in eighty days, as Phineas Fogg had done, not in seventy-five days, as she had promised, but in a little more than seventy-two days.

No era of swift airplane and luxurious transportation can understand the true significance of Nellie Bly's pioneer achievement. Since time began, no one had made a trip around the world in anywhere near so short a time.

Mayor Cleveland of Jersey City shoved his way through the hysterical mob and tried to make himself heard. The people quieted to listen to his speech.

"The American girl can no longer be misunderstood," he cried out. "She will be recognized as pushing, determined, independent, able to take care of herself wherever she may go. You have added another spark to the great beacon light of American liberty, that is leading the people of other nations in the grand march of civilization and progress. Passing rapidly by them, you have cried out in a language they could all understand, 'Forward!' and you have made it the watchword of 1890. The American people from every part of this great and glorious country shout back to you, 'Forward!' and God speed you on your wonderful march!"

Then the crowds moved in again, snatching for souvenirs Nell's gloves and handkerchief, pleading for autographs. The Mayor tried to outshout them as he continued: "Forward! It is the very essence and spirit of the age and times in which we live. People the world over have been taught that they are not as far apart as they imagined. You have set the whole world to thinking about it and so have brought mankind closer together. Welcome home—Nellie Bly!"

Eventually Nell had to extricate herself from her frenzied admirers. As she bowed and smiled, her voice rose clear and triumphant:

"From Jersey to Jersey is around the world. And I am in Jersey now!"

In New York more crowds were waiting. Mobs followed Nell's carriage all the way to Park Row. Cortlandt Street, West Street, Fulton Street were black seas of people. They hung from windows, stood on overturned horsecars, blocked traffic, and brought Nell's carriage to a standstill time after time.

At 4:30 P.M. Nell's carriage reached the *World* headquarters. Ten cannons boomed from the Battery and Fort Green Park, Brooklyn. Then Nell was brought to the nearby Astor House for a champagne reception.

Nell raised her glass, her face radiant.

"It was all wonderful, especially the last lap. If the success of my trip had depended on English trains, I would still be sitting, wrapped in a rug, my feet on a warmer, looking at San Francisco. American trains, fortunately, are a thousand per cent ahead of European trains. They are cleaner, faster, better run. An American train got me home on time." She looked about and laughed at the wonder of all that was happening to her.

"I feel like a successful presidential candidate," said Nellie Bly.

FATHER TIME OUTDONE!

Even Imagination's Record Pales Before the Performance of "The World's" Globe-Circler.

HER TIME: 72 DAYS, 6 HRS., 11 MIN., -- SEC.

Thousands Cheer Themselves Hoarse at Nellie Bly's Arrival.

WELCOME SALUTES IN NEW YORK AND BROOKLYN.

The Whole Country Aglow with Intense Enthusiasm.

NELLIE BLY TELLS HER STORY.

Courtesy of The New York Historical Society, New York City.

FATHER TIME OUTDONE! screamed next morning's headlines in the *World*. "Even imagination's record pales before the performance of the *World's* Globe Circler!"

In America, and in Paris, London, and Berlin, Nellie Bly, "the toast of five continents," was on everyone's lips. Jules Verne cabled: "I never doubted the success of Nellie Bly. She has proved her intrepidity and courage. Hurrah for her and for the Director of the *World!* Hurrah! Hurrah!"

In France, although no French girl would have dared to try such an unconventional feat as going around the world alone, the newspapers were for the most part favorable. *Figaro* pronounced Nell's achievement "Prodigious! Extraordinary!"

The London papers, which had been predicting Nell's failure from the start, now did an about face: "It is an idea none but an American girl could successfully have carried out."

In Berlin, Professor Verchow, president of the Anthropological Society, said, beaming, "I consider Miss Bly's trip a great achievement and admire her pluck." Professor Baron von Rechtzofer, president of the Geographical Society, was also elated. He said that Nellie Bly had really begun something, and that other record breakers would come along thick and fast.

Pittsburgh sent its greetings to the *World*. "Accept our congratulations on the success of your globe-girdling enterprise and present the compliments of the *Commercial Gazette* to the fair Nellie. There is a warm place in the heart of all Pittsburgh for her."

The Pittsburgh Order of Elks proceeded to elect her an honorary member. Down in Tennessee, Nell was deeded a large tract of land. A race horse was named after her, and she was asked to endorse everything from cigars to travelers' checks. The ghillie cap she had worn on her round-the-world jaunt became famous overnight as the "Nellie Bly cap," and was the rage with fashionable women everywhere.

P. T. Barnum cabled: "As an American who knows by experience the difficulties and dangers of travel, I congratulate Miss Bly of the *World* on her most remarkable success, personal pluck, and courage. From the great amount of public attention she is attracting both at home and abroad, I look in her direction for new popular features in my show."

And the Geographic Society of New York asked: "What next for Nell—the moon?"

Nellie Bly went home to her uptown flat to rest for a few days, pose for photographers, and think over offers from syndicates and from managers of lecture tours. Her monkey at once broke all the dishes in her kitchen and so, reluctantly, Nell bequeathed him to the Central Park Zoo.

The first excitement over, Nell asked the explanation of the appearance in Hong Kong of a rival reporter. The *World* knew nothing about her. The mystery however, was cleared up a bit later. When news of Nell's trip around the world leaked out, a woman writer had been hastily recruited, not by the *World*, but by a national magazine, to outdo Nellie

WILL IT COME TO THIS?

The Kind of Reception Our Enterprising Friends Are Apparently Arranging for "The World's" Globe-Girdling Tourist.

Courtesy of The New York Public Library, New York City.

Bly. But, although much money was spent and influence exerted to bring her in first on a west-to-east race around the world, the lady missed a ship at Le Havre and found that the North German Lloyd steamer which she had expected to catch had been withdrawn. She arrived back in New York without fanfare.

The *World* announced that Nell was taking a "well-earned vacation" from her regular assignments, and she embarked on a forty-week lecture tour around America. In the same gown she had worn during her globe-trotting trip, Nell made her New York première, her dark eyes glowing, her voice young and dramatic, telling her stories to standing-room audiences, as only Nell could tell them.

With her newspaper earnings, syndicate work, lectures, and testimonials for everything from Morse's pills to typewriters, Nellie Bly earned, from then on, a reputed twenty-five thousand dollars a year. A fabulous sum for a woman of her day. Her face was now the best known face in America. And nightly the Moulton Opera Company, in their operetta *The Black Hussar*, sang:

> Jules Verne declared in eighty days
> A man the trip could do,
> Along trots Nellie Bly and does
> The job in seventy-two.
>
> I wonder when they'll send a girl
> To travel round the sky,
> Read the answer in the stars,
> They wait for Nellie Bly.

CHAPTER XIX

NOT-SO-GAY NINETIES

WHAT did a girl do when she had become the most talked-about, the most sought-after young woman in the world?

The triumphant return was over, the lecture tours with their throngs of admiring fans were past. Fine clothes and many admirers had become part of the regular routine. But, though Nell's spirit remained gay, in many respects she had grown very serious. She felt older and wiser than the men who escorted her—men who took her to the opera to hear Emma Eames, or to the theater to see Julia Marlowe or Lillian Russell, or drove with her in a carriage past Trinity Church, speaking of its beauty while she thought of the disgraceful slums which lurked in its shadow. With printer's ink in her blood, she had to go on asking her searching questions and writing her pieces to better the world. But what about her personal life? In spite of countless proposals, Nell could not make up her mind about marriage.

What did a girl do? Nellie Bly had still to find out.

SHE'S HOME AGAIN!

Life's Greatest Enterprise.

Our Peerless Sadie Beats the Record.

She Meets Some Noted People and Observes Some Strange Occurrences.

—Life is a Great Journal.

MISS SADIE, BEFORE STARTING.

About three o'clock yesterday morning, just as our staff was working to get the Chinese edition of LIFE to press, a dull roar was heard coming up West Twenty-third Street. The staff rushed to the windows as one man. Imagine our pride and joy when we distinguished a crowd of distinguished citizens, shouting themselves hoarse with cheers for LIFE and Sadie McGinty. On a shutter borne on the shoulders of Chauncey M. Depew, Ward McAllister, William M. Evarts and Jay Gould stood the brave girl, her now-famous sachel in her hand and a smile of conscious merit on her face. Preceding her were three hand-organs, playing "Home Again" in unison. As the crowd stopped in front of LIFE office, loud huzzas rent the skies and then rented the buildings across the street.

MISS SADIE MEETS ALBERT EDWARD.

MISS SADIE AND THE G. O. M.

Kissing her hand to the crowd, Sadie leaped gracefully from the shutter and through the portals of the office. Immediately on her arrival in the sanctum three editorial writers proposed marriage, which propositions Miss Sadie now has under consideration.

"I am so glad to be back," she said, and a silvery laugh rattled through her pearly teeth.

"How do you like America, Miss Sadie?" we asked.

"Much better than Chicago," she replied; "but it really doesn't compare with Harlem. My trip from the latter place to the Battery was one complete ovation. I reached Hester Street just in time to witness the annual out-door games. They were not very exciting, as only four men and a policeman were killed."

"Did you use any of the letters of introduction which you took away with you?"

"As I came through Baxter Street I learned that Col. Elliot F. Shepard was giving a reception to the Prince of Wales at McCloskeY's Hall. Remembering that I had a letter of introduction from Russell Harrison, I presented it. We sat together three hours in the conservatory, and he assured me that just as soon as he could go to Chicago and secure a divorce from the Princess he would ask me to be his, provided LIFE would pay his debts.

"'And how is Russ? and what a dear, dear fellow he is!' said the Prince, turning to me impulsively. 'And, my dear Miss Sadie, you must fail not to stop at Paradise Park and see Mr. Gladstone.'

"I thought this a good suggestion and stopped off. The Grand Old Man had been advised of my coming and went through the usual business of permitting me to surprise him cutting down a property tree with a *papier-maché* axe."

"Did you have any conversation with him?"

"Oh, yes; he said a number of brilliant things, but I discovered afterward that they were stolen from 'Robert Elsmere' and Marie Bashkirtseff's Journal. As I left him

he pressed my hand and shouted after me, 'Erin go Bragh!'"

For the benefit of those interested in our guessing match we would state that the exact time of Miss Sadie's return was 3.35.36 A.M.

At the request of many of LIFE's readers—our circulation last week being 100,000,001½ copies—we have concluded to give Miss Sadie a public reception, where they may have the pleasure of meeting the courageous little lady in person. We have engaged the Metropolitan Opera House for that purpose. Owing to other engagements, Mr. Ward McAllister will not be able to act as Master of Ceremonies, but Mr. John L. Sullivan has kindly consented to act in that capacity. Carriages will approach by Eleventh Avenue and no wine will be served after 6 A.M. For the convenience of the Four Hundred, Colonel Shepard will allow the Fifth Avenue stages to run all night. Babies in arms will not be admitted unless in

ANNUAL OUT-DOOR GAMES OF THE HESTER STREET AMATEUR ATHLETIC ASSOCIATION.

full evening dress and accompanied by adults. Come one, come all!

James Metcalfe, Nellie's friend and the editor of *Life*, gaily satirized her round-the-world tour in *Life*.

There were ceaseless rumors about her romances and many of them were true. A favored admirer was her man of the blizzard, James Metcalfe, one of the Harvard alumni who had helped to found in 1883 the gently satirical *Life* magazine. He had beaued Nellie around even before her trip, met her in Philadelphia on her return, and gaily spoofed her round-the-world tour in a series in his magazine featuring the adventures of "Miss Sadie McGinty, *Life's* celebrated and fearless reporter," in a trip around Manhattan Island.

"My instructions from *Life*," the invincible Sadie had written, "were to discover the North Pole, if I could do so without varying too much from the route as originally laid out. I have the pleasure to report that I discovered it in front of a First Avenue barbershop and that it now bears *Life's* card of advertising rates, a statement that *Life's* circulation last week was 46,956,431½ copies, and your correspondent's name."

When Nellie Bly returned in triumph from her trip, Sadie McGinty, with only a black eye to denote her harrowing experiences in Harlem, was also applauded. "Kissing her hand to the crowd," *Life* reported, "Sadie leaped gracefully from a shutter through the portals of the office. Immediately on her arrival in the sanctum three editorial writers proposed marriage, which propositions Miss McGinty now has under consideration."

But regardless of the spoofing, Metcalfe had a very serious interest in Nellie Bly. They went together everywhere and a verse of his, published in *Life,* clearly referred to their first meeting.

> Dainty maid, fair maid, your name I fain would know
> For every time I look at you, more sorrowful I grow.
> When first you dropped upon the pave and I came walking by
> I picked you up and looked at you with far from eager eye.
> But this soon changed to interest and then to something more
> Until at last, I now must own, a woman I adore!

The handsome Mr. Metcalfe was a dashing suitor, and her friend, Erasmus Wilson in Pittsburgh, had been dependable. James Whitcomb Riley had written a verse about Erasmus:

> 'Ras Wilson, I respect you cause
> You're common like you always was
> Afore you went to town and s'prised
> The world by getting recognized,
> And yet preservin' as they say
> Your common horse sense every way.

But perhaps the fame and fortune of Nellie Bly had discouraged Erasmus; perhaps the difference in their ages had frightened him away. He had not met Nellie in Pittsburgh. He had not come to New York. But there were plenty to take his place.

Her questions unanswered, Nell flung herself into her work.

She had spent part of her sabbatical leave doing articles for a weekly magazine. She returned to the *World* in September, 1893, a celebrated personality in the American tradition of Horatio Alger. She had gone from rags to riches, from obscurity to fame.

Known far and wide as a "stunt" or personality girl, much was made of this side of her character by the *World*. But her true genius was as an investigator, and, as the problems of capital and labor came more and more to the front during the America of the nineties, Nellie Bly with her experience and understanding was a natural for appraising them.

She launched a Sunday column, an innovation on a newspaper. It was embellished with a sketch of a dark-eyed thoughtful maiden in decorative sailor hat, encircled in a bower of flowers. In other sketches, she appeared as a Salvation Army lass, or boxing with Gentleman Jim Corbett, champion fighter of the world.

Without gloves she took on the major problems of America, one by one.

It was an America of vast resources, increasing prestige abroad, and growing pains at home that Nellie Bly surveyed in her office, now housed under the shining gold dome of the new World Building. Far from being merely the Gay Nineties, a time when the daughters of the rich were being married off at a great rate to titled Europeans, a time of glittering theater and ostentatious society life, it was a period also of stress and strain. It might well have been called the Turbulent Nineties.

This was a period of new discoveries, of great truths revealed, said a *World* editorial of 1894. Germs were being

Nellie Bly's Sunday column was an innovation in newspaper publishing in 1893.

NELLIE BLY'S
COLUMN.

This is all my own. Herein every Sunday I may say all I please and what I please.

Courtesy of The New York Public Library, New York City.

identified for what they were; serum was being given for dreaded tuberculosis; people were learning to sterilize milk by boiling it; infant mortality was lessening; improved sanitary conditions were bringing about a decrease, in America at least, of cholera and typhoid fever.

An increasing number of employers were voluntarily trying to improve the conditions of their employees, and standards of living were higher. Yet cheap labor brought in from abroad was stirring up trouble with native workers, and too many employers were still as blind to human needs of workmen as workmen were blind to the pressures upon employers.

"Nothing pays better in business than decency," the *World* declared when, following one of the many strikes of that era, eleven thousand clockmakers returned to work after resolving their differences with the management amicably and fairly.

With a strong individualistic middle class, there was some difference of opinion as to how to reach that "life, liberty, and pursuit of happiness" every American felt to be his heritage. But at least most people agreed about food and ate heartily. A newspaper menu for Sunday dinner disclosed that the middle-class citizen might enjoy: Mock Turtle Soup, Fricasseed Flounder, Small Creamed Potatoes, Beefsteak with Cucumbers and Onion, Sweet Potato au Caramel, Corn Salad with French Dressing, Waffles, Cheese, Apple Croquettes, and Coffee!

The *World,* along with many thinking Americans, was opposed to haphazard, unrestricted immigration. Hordes of bewildered ignorant newcomers continued to pour into already badly crowded cities, adding slums to slums and pulling down the standards of urban living. Although a Democrat sheet, the *World* also was opposed, along with the prominent Presbyterian reformer of that era Dr. Charles Parkhurst, to "graft-ridden Tammany Hall," with its attending police corruption, protected gambling, and prostitution dens, some within a stone's throw of Dr. Parkhurst's New York church. Likewise, it was against ruthless business tactics employed by rich "robber barons," and wanted the breaking up of huge trusts and more equal distribution of wealth.

The paper sparked the growing public censure. Change began slowly but surely. Multimillionaires, among them John D. Rockefeller Sr., and Andrew Carnegie, began developing a social conscience, pouring back part of their vast fortunes into libraries and philanthropic enterprises for the benefit of the people. "The man who dies rich, dies disgraced," said Scottish-born Carnegie in a Pittsburgh speech reported in the *World* in 1894, and some years later added this footnote: "Wealth cannot stave off trouble and death."

Then came the Panic of 1893—the closing of three hundred banks, the failure of fifteen thousand business firms, innumerable farmers losing homes on small mortgages, and hundreds of thousands becoming unemployed in large cities. Disaster ran riot. The *World* gave away bread in New York City, the Salvation Army opened soup kitchens, and governmental relief for the unemployed was provided for the first time. America was in crisis, but meeting that crisis.

"America is better off than most countries," commented the *World*, "particularly Germany, India, Russia, South America, Armenia, and embalmed, dying China."

Yet tension between Japan and China was fast building toward war in Korea the following year.

Labor troubles in America brought about an upsurge of Anarchists, radicals, and the lunatic fringe, who called on "the common man to strike out against the Capitalist and bring about an international brotherhood of man."

"Jimmy, the newsboy," sized up the Anarchist's philosophy in an observation for the *World*: "Anarchy is sort of free graft for everyone. Anarchists don' pay nothin' and wanter kill people what do."

The general public grew indignant over "dangerous radicals, troublesome foreigners, unwashed Russians and Poles, and beer-drinking Germans," whose fierce oratory was sometimes punctuated by bomb-throwings and strychnine poisonings.

One assignment of Nellie's on her return to the *World* was to interview the "queen of the Anarchists," Russian-born Emma Goldman, who was languishing in jail for inciting riot. Nellie Bly saw her there in late September, 1893. Nell, a Republican by sentiment only, since she had no vote, was surprised, and honest enough to say so, when she found that Emma did not look her part.

"You see her in your mind as a great raw-boned creature," wrote Nell, "short hair and bloomers, red flag in one hand, burning torch in the other, feet constantly off the ground and 'murder' continually on her lips." But what Nell found was "a tiny girl just five feet high, weighing 120 pounds, with a saucy turned-up nose, blue-gray eyes, shell-rimmed glasses, and a copy of *Illustrated America* in her hand. She had light brown hair and strong white teeth. She wore a blue serge Eton suit, blue shirtwaist, and a scarf."

Emma told Nell: "I have been an Anarchist all my life. I am one because I am an egotist. It pains me to see others suffer. I cannot bear it. I never hurt a man in my life. And I don't think I could. So, because what others suffer makes me suffer, I am an Anarchist and give my life for my cause, for only through it can be ended all suffering, want, and unhappiness. Everything wrong—crime and sickness—are the result of the system under which we live. Were there no Capitalists, people would not be overworked, starved and ill-housed, made old before their time, diseased, and made criminals. The Anarchists build the best of everything."

"What, for example?" Nell demanded.

"Take the Broadway cable, New York's new trolley, for instance. Instead of running few cars at frightful speed in order to save expense, we should run many cars at slow speed, and so prevent accidents."

"If you do away with money and employers," asked practical Nell, "who will work upon your railroads?"

"Those who like that kind of work. Everyone should do that which he likes best, not a thing that he is compelled to do to earn his daily bread."

"What would you do with the lazy ones who would not work?"

"No one is lazy," said Emma positively. "They grow hopeless from the misery of their existence and give up. Under *our* order of things, every man would do the work he liked best and would have as much as his neighbor, so could not be unhappy and discouraged."

"What would you do with the criminals, if everyone is free and prisons unheard of?"

"We believe that with the liquidation of Capitalists we would not have a criminal. Why are there criminals today? Because some have everything, others nothing. Under our system every man would be equal. To steal there must be something to steal. We do not grant there is anything to steal, for everything should be free."

Nell said, "We look upon marriage as a cornerstone of society. You do not believe in marriage. What do you propose shall take its place?"

Emma's gray eyes clouded.

"I believe in the marriage of affection. That is the only true marriage. If two people care for each other, they have a right to live together as long as that love exists. When it is dead, what base immorality for them still to stay together! Let there be nothing but voluntary affection and there ceases to exist the prostitute wife and the prostitute street woman."

"But children?" protested Nell. "What would you do with them? Men would desert; women and children would be left uncared for and destitute."

"On the contrary, then men would never desert. If a couple decided to separate, there would be public homes and schools for the children. Mothers who would rather do something other than care for children could put them in schools, where they would be cared for by women who preferred taking care of children to anything else in life. In this way, we would never have diseased or disabled children from careless and incompetent mothers."

"Do you think that murder is going to help your cause?" Nell asked bluntly.

Emma shook her head. "I don't believe that through murder we shall gain. Only by War—Labor against Capital, Masses against Classes."

A strong advocate of reform, Nell published Emma Goldman's theories even though she disagreed with them.

As unemployment and a drought in the West continued to disrupt the nation, another champion of the people arose in the person of Jacob Sechler Coxey. He was a wealthy Ohio businessman, a Populist. Seeking legislation for public works to give employment to the idle, he proposed large issues of legal tender currency. In 1894, he organized a "living petition of unemployed" who marched on Washington to ask the enactment of remedial legislation. Larger "industrial armies" from other sections of the country, particularly the Far West, were to join him and form Coxey's Army. But they disbanded before reaching the capital, and only twelve hundred haggard men straggled into Washington. On May Day, fewer than five hundred were on hand to parade in what the *World* described as "Coxey's Farce."

The rest had been lost through disease and desertion and death.

Nelly Bly had come to Washington to cover the story. She had gone to the campsite where the "Commonweal Army" was barricaded, and found the army made up mostly of farm boys in their teens who had wanted to see America. The living conditions were filthy; the water was polluted; there were no sanitary provisions; the men slept on dirty rags on the ground and, excepting for the day of the big parade, were fed on scraps. The morning of the parade, Coxey saw to it that they got one square meal of boiled eggs, coffee, ham, and bread. Coxey and Carl Browne, one of his adjutants who proclaimed himself to be "the reincarnated Christ," never came near the site; they were too busy, Nell found, "making speeches ranting against the Capitalists." But they were charging admission to the public to see the plight to which they claimed the government was subjecting the men, selling photos, and pocketing the fees.

As Nell went about talking to the boys, she found hardly one skilled workman in the lot.

"They seemed to have a hazy notion that work would be provided for all," wrote Nell. "If Browne and Coxey love these men, as they pretend, how can they sleep on springs and hair mattresses in fine hotels, knowing their followers are lying on hard ground on piles of filth? If it were love that prompted their movement and if they were martyrs for America's downtrodden workmen, they would eat what their followers eat, sleep where they sleep, and share with them, step by step, the hard journey they persuaded them to make."

Christopher Columbus Jones, another adjutant of "General" Coxey, did appear at the campsite to get the main body of the parade under way. He knew Nell was a reporter, but had not yet discovered she was the famous Nellie Bly. Since she was a good-looking girl, and this segment of the parade sadly needed a little "class," he told her, "You can lead the parade if you wish. Stop occasionally to review it; then take the lead again."

THE PHOTOGRAPH TAKEN JUST BEFORE THE PROCESSION WAS FORMED.

Courtesy of The New York Public Library, New York City.

Nell, who was most anxious to catch up with "General" Coxey, replied, "That suits me exactly."

Pennsylvania Avenue was lined with curious crowds as the fantastic procession of half-starved Commonwealers straggled past. After a "triumphal march" down the avenue, the parade as it neared the Capitol was turned back by mounted police.

Nell found "General" Coxey seated in his chaise beside his wife and infant child, widely advertised under the name, "Little Legal Tender."

The day before, Coxey had been told by Speaker Crisp that he could present all the petitions he liked to Congress as an American citizen, but, that if he appeared on the Capitol steps to make a speech and incite riot, he would be arrested. Coxey had told the senator that he represented the entire nation, and Crisp had retorted:

"How do you, one man, speak for sixty-five million people?"

Coxey told him that he was "the people's representative" and that "presenting a petition to Congress and waiting for the ballot is too slow for me." He had threatened that unless the government took immediate action on his program, there would be a revolution and bloodshed.

Now, as Coxey jumped out of his chaise, his wife broke out sobbing. Nell saw that his breezy manner did not cover his fear. His nearsighted blue eyes peered out timidly from behind big round glasses and he shook like an ague victim.

As he scurried over the green grass of the Capitol grounds toward the steps waving a roll of manuscript, two bluecoats jumped him. Several of his companions grappled with the police and were promptly hauled off to jail.

"With more politeness than New York police would accord him," Nell related, Mr. Coxey was permitted to hustle back to his carriage.

"Are you satisfied with today's work?" Nellie Bly asked Coxey, when she finally buttonholed him.

"Perfectly," he said shakily.

"What are you going to do now?" Nell wanted to know.

"Stay here. If the men must starve, let the government see them do it."

"How did you first get the idea about this business?"

Coxey beamed. "I conceived the plan about good roads. Then I dreamed up non-interest-bearing bonds. That is the greatest idea that was ever placed before the American public."

Nellie Bly eyed him in amazement, wondering who he thought would pay for all his schemes. In her story she wrote: "I believe in the workingmen. I believe they are strong and powerful enough to right their wrongs in a dignified way, without the aid of selfish and greedy schemers. Poor Commonwealers. I hope they won't consent to starve much longer for the glorification and gain of self-seekers. God speed them back to their homes, to family and fortune is the wish of a friend—Nellie Bly."

But increasing unemployment and labor troubles in America were causing real concern. Adding fuel to the fires of the Anarchists and Commonwealer leaders came Eugene Debs, Socialist candidate for President. He, more than the others, was reported to have been instrumental in inciting riots and strikes all over the nation, particularly among the railroad workers of Chicago and New York. With a just cause to start with, for experienced workers unquestionably were underpaid and overworked, the excesses he was rumored to have encouraged turned the general public against him. On July 9, 1894, President Cleveland issued a proclamation to the striking Pullman rioters in Chicago. It declared martial law, and United States troops moved in. The following day the mob retaliated by setting fire to some Illinois Central freight cars.

Nellie Bly arrived in Chicago on July 11 to look the strike situation over. Her sympathies were with the Pullman officials. She had heard much about Pullman, Illinois, the model town just outside Chicago. And she had small use for champions of the people who fomented strikes and prescribed endless privation for their followers while keeping up their own spirits on full stomachs, good liquor, and clean beds. But she was determined to get at the truth, if possible.

The "scab" railroad conductor reluctantly agreed to take her out to the model town, but advised Nell not to go, for trouble might break out any minute. Even with United States troops around, he told her, he himself would not dare make the trip after dark. Outside agitators had come in to keep the strike going, and all the residents who were able to were sending their families away.

Nell rode right along with him on a two-decker car, the

sole passenger. She asked, "Does Mr. Pullman ever ride out here on this car?"

"No, he never did. The vice-president and the other officers do though."

"What is the main cause of dissatisfaction among the men?"

"Low wages."

"But business is bad. Mr. Pullman only had one order in his shop for a hundred elevated trains for New York City when the strike broke."

"We know that. But the workers feel that, when wages are cut, rents should be cut too."

Nell nodded approval.

Her first sight of the model town was quite favorable. Although built on a sand hill, the houses lining the railroad were clean and neat. But once she got off the car and stepped behind the stage front, she found squalor and misery. For every neatly kept home with flower garden, she saw numerous wretched ill-kept rooms with broken-down furniture, dirt, flies, and scores of undernourished children. Rents were higher in Pullman Town than elsewhere; a tax of fifty cents a mounth was levied on homes with shutters; those unable to pay their rents were evicted with no place to go.

Still, as she went the rounds, she was told in every kind of accent that only a few workmen wanted to strike, even though they felt they had deep grievances. She glanced about one fly-infested tenement. A tired woman in bare feet nursed an ailing baby, while her striking husband stared at his empty larder. The committee for the strikers had given them coffee, half a pound of sugar, and two loaves of bread that day, but, with a family of eight to feed, this did not go far.

"I didn't strike," the man told Nell defensively, while his wife glared at him accusingly. "I didn't know no more about it than you did till I came out the gate after working hours and saw a notice posted up. But now if we starve we won't go back. An' I 'ave a family of eight!"

"You are surely not blaming Mr. Pullman because of the size of your family?" Nell asked good-naturedly.

"No. But it's 'ungry we are. 'Ungry we get up, an' 'ungry we go to bed, while the men w'at ordered us out an' the millionaires w'at employed us get along as well as ever. If that Master Debs would only take time off before 'e goes to 'is hotel dinner to remember us as 'ave stomachs an' get 'ungry too. . . ."

During the next few days Nellie Bly endeared herself to the strikers and their families. Being of a practical turn of mind and endowed with a conscience, she began pulling wires to get food to this starving town. In addition, she did many personal and unrecorded good deeds. The longer she stayed, the more popular Nell became. Ministers, strikers, strikebreakers, wives, and children all talked freely to her. They recognized that this girl whose brains and hard work had taken her so far was not in the least afraid of getting her white sailor hat smeared with grime and fly specks while she championed other humans less able to cope with life than she was!

Nell saw no fierce firebrands here, no murders, rioters, and wild-eyed Anarchists. She saw countless hungry, dispirited men and women with helpless children, who had reason to expect more from their labor than they were getting.

"I had come to Chicago," wrote Nell, "bitterly set against strikes. And as far as I could understand, the inhabitants of the model town hadn't a reason to complain. I intended to denounce the rioters. But in half a day I was with them. If ever men and women have reason to strike, those men and women have. I find wrongs everywhere."

But if Nell was disillusioned with Pullman she was elated to find that there was a real model town in America. It was Leclaire, Illinois, located an hour's distance from St. Louis, Missouri. Significantly, no agitators were able to incite a strike in this town.

Unlike Pullman, Leclaire did not present its best side to the railroad tracks, but only the backs of its houses, seemingly indifferent to what passers-by thought of them. But, as Nell became acquainted with the town, she was charmed.

"It is a simple, pretty town," she wrote. "The longer you stay here, the more you like it. The streets are not laid out in checkerboard fashion; they wind this way and that, with artistic irregularity. Each house is individual in design; each has large windows and one third of an acre of land. The only conformity is in that everything and everybody look clean, happy, and prosperous.

"The factory which supported the town was centrally located, with garden and high hedge separating it from the home sections. It was a beautiful building with modern fire sprinklers, electric fans, electric lights, and steam heat."

Leclaire had been founded by a modest man named N. O. Nelson, Nell wrote. Unlike Pullman, he did not name the town after himself, nor did he hold himself apart from the workers. Though he lived on a farm, he was part of this community; he knew the children by name and was loved by them. He had named the town after an equally unassuming Frenchman who had founded a profit-sharing business near Paris, fifty years before.

Nelson had been a farm boy and soldier who began work in a manufacturing house in St. Louis. In 1877, he had started the N. O. Nelson Manufacturing Company with only an honest heart and "a pocketful of quarters" as assets. He had selected a 125-acre site in a healthy location with good well water, cheap coal and convenience to the city as drawing features and brought a few people to work and live there.

"He doesn't believe in wholesale cooperative plans," reported Nell. "In the factory, the same wages are paid as outside Leclaire; the motto is 'Individual Independence.' Workmen can live here or elsewhere; they can buy or rent as they please; they can join the profit-sharing plan, or not. They can go away and come back and share in the profits just the same, provided they invest one-tenth their earnings in the business. They can sell their stock if they quit. When times are bad, the men mutually agree to change the working day from nine to ten hours, and there is no wage decrease. If a man falls ill, payments on his house are declared off until he is well again; meanwhile, the provident committee takes care of his family."

Nell wished Emma Goldman might have visited Leclaire.

So the adventuress became the crusader again, the good angel of the laboring classes, the tenement houses, and factories, the enemy of corrupt politicians, the confidante of the meek and the mighty. Nell visited Saratoga's gambling dens and exposed frauds and swindlers who preyed upon the public. She did a series of political exposés as part of the *World's* campaign to oust the then corrupt Tammany machine from power in New York City. She was sent to a Democratic convention to interview the Tammany chiefs who were under fire. The *World* condemned them for their spoils system, ruthless blackmailing, buying votes, protecting gambling, and prostitution. Tammany wished to be known as the friend of the downtrodden. It always gave picnic lunches for the poor just before voting time. But some of its leaders did have a real understanding and sympathy for the poor. Nell went to the convention certain she would be annihilated. But the First Tiger, Speaker Sulzer, took a fancy to her and they became friends. When she said, "What a pretty badge you have on," he took it off and fastened it to her jacket. It was a blue ribbon which said in gold letters:

> Tammany Hall
> Saratoga
> Oct. 5, 1893.

"I'm robbing you. And I will still have to tell the truth in my story," Nell protested.

"That's all right," said Speaker Sulzer. Nell wore the badge, then asked questions which embarrassed even the toughest of the leaders and went home to write colorful personality stories on the Tammany crowd. The *World* backed the stories with a cartoon showing a subdued Tammany tiger being led away on a chain by a gay and determined Nellie Bly.

NELLIE BLY AND THE CAPTURED TIGER.

Courtesy of The New York Public Library, New York City.

Nell also did several more interviews with Dr. Charles Parkhurst, who had earlier appreciated her help in his campaign to clean up New York. He was now to refer to her as his ablest aid in bringing about reform in America.

The flaming young reporter was maturing. As she did so, she developed all the characteristics necessary for her work—earnestness combined with a sense of human fairmindedness, a progressive spirit, a determination amounting to genius, a compassionate heart. Her exposure of frauds, incompetent and dishonest public officials, and abuses in public institutions and her defense of the poor against the rich and powerful made her a nightmare in the lives of shady dealers, and the darling of the people. Her assignments in the line of public service began to put her in the ranks of the best American journalists.

It should have been enough for any girl. But Nell was a woman now. She was approaching her twenty-eighth birthday. And there was something lacking.

"What do you really want out of life?" Erasmus Wilson had asked that day in Pittsburgh so long ago, when she had talked of coming to New York. She could remember his voice, his look. Had they held disappointment? She thought of his words:

"Crash a New York paper, reform the world, fall in love, and marry a millionaire!"

She had done the first, given all she had to the second. Had she found the third was not for her? The *World* and the world speculated about Nellie Bly and James Metcalfe.

But, when she stopped seeing him, her quiet smile and hazel eyes told them nothing.

All that was left was a millionaire. But Nell had money of her own, as money went, and wealthy admirers aplenty. She had always refused her millionaires.

What next, Nellie Bly? The public waited and wondered.

CHAPTER XX

MARRY A MILLIONAIRE

It was eight below zero and a bitter wind was blowing as
Nell got up at three o'clock in the morning to take a train
out of Valentine, Nebraska. She climbed aboard a dirty
cheerless car and, though she wore a sealskin coat, a golf
cape, hood, and carried a rug, she was chilled. She was also
lonely. Not for people; the car was full of them—noisy, chat-
tering, rude. But for someone who would be concerned
about Nell.

For once in her life Nellie Bly did not feel independent.
She had been visiting the stricken areas of the West, where
two summers of drought, followed by harsh winters, had
left hundreds destitute in Nebraska and South Dakota. She
was not her usual bright and vivid self.

Was her life going to prove too much for her? she wondered, as she curled up on the dusty plush seat. She had
seen countless newspaper men, unable to stand pressures
of the business they could not leave, drink themselves into
oblivion or work themselves to death in a few years. Even
the great Joseph Pulitzer had sacrificed all in pursuit of
tomorrow's headlines. And Nell? How many times had she
risen in a dismal dawn to go somewhere? how many trains

241

had she taken? how many deadlines had she met? only to be faced with others—always a new one coming up! Thousands of ideas had come from her busy brain, millions of words from her racing pen. Yet always the hungry presses demanded more. If tomorrow her pen failed her, what then?

What would be the end of it? In her personal life her standards had remained Victorian. At twenty-five a girl was an old maid; at thirty . . .

Nell stared out of the window at the frozen landscape, the blighted land with dead cattle seemingly strewn everywhere. The scene was as bleak as her heart.

But she covered the Western assignment with the same resolution and compassion as always. She interviewed innumerable gaunt ranchers living in Russian-type sod houses they had built when their homes had been destroyed the previous summer by prairie fires. She wrote of them and the longing for a home which had brought them here, to a place where they had sunk all their money in land and crops that had failed them. She went with Major Crager, the U.S. agent, to visit an Indian encampment within fifty yards of a Nebraska hotel. The braves were languid from starvation but a squaw was putting up a teepee.

In temperatures of twenty below and with icicles forming on her clothing, Nell rode to the hut of a bachelor rancher. It was a hole in the ground, where only one man could stand upright. She sat on a box, the one article of furniture. The rancher's clothing was in rags. His bed was straw covered with more rags. He had a pan, a primitive stove, and that was all except for a violin which hung pathetically from the roof pole.

"What do you have to eat?" Nell asked him.

"Bread and milk, right now. I traded a pig for the last sack of flour."

"It's good you have a cow."

He sighed. "She's mortgaged. They'll come and get her tomorrow."

His story was the story of them all. He had started with five hundred dollars, came out here, staked a claim, built a little house and a barn. The first year his crop had been fine. The second summer rain, hail, and hell had overtaken him and all his money went for seed. The third summer brought the prairie fire.

With her paper's backing, Nell arranged that a relief committee be set up in the East, to send food and serum and doctors to this stricken place. When her mission was finally accomplished, aid pouring in and promises with it, promises of new homes, new schools, and new hope, Nellie Bly, more tired than she had ever felt in her life, started on her trip back East.

She got on the Chicago-bound special and moved toward the only unoccupied seat in the car. She wore a smart suit and fashionable hat with twin wings adorning it. Interested eyes followed her sophisticated figure. Interested eyes always followed Nellie Bly and always would. She was still pretty, though the look of first youth was gone and there were shadows of fatigue under her hazel eyes. Her bangs had disappeared; her dark hair was now parted in the center and arranged at the nape of her neck in the chignon style of the moment. But, although there was a look of recognition on many faces, Nell was no longer stopped, as she once had been, with requests for her autograph.

She took the empty seat next to a nice-looking man of obvious years and distinction, impeccably groomed, with a strong profile. He looked like a diplomat or a statesman, Nell thought absently. It was a relief to have a gentleman for a seat companion; she had run up against some rough characters in her Western travels.

She removed her hat, smoothed her hair, and leaned back against the seat. Her head ached; she felt a desperate need for quiet and rest. In a few moments she was asleep.

When she awoke, her headache was gone. The man beside her was reading a newspaper and she saw with a start of pleasure that it was her paper, the *World*. He was reading one of her stories on the Western drought, with the headline "Nellie Bly Roughing It." Finally he removed his glasses, put down his paper, and flushed a little when he saw that she was awake.

"Forgive me for intruding. But I couldn't help noticing—I must ask you—are you Nellie Bly?"

Nell nodded and he broke into a smile. "I have seen your photographs. And for years I've followed your brilliant career. I have wanted so much to have the pleasure of meeting you."

He handed her his card. It read, "Robert Seaman, Esquire."

Nellie had heard all that he had said a thousand times before, and as many times had deftly evaded such flattery, had eluded rosy-cheeked schoolboys and gushing girls, doting mothers with promising prodigies, society women, politicians, cranks, titled foreigners, garrulous old men. But this man, though much her senior, did not seem old, nor someone to elude. She liked him, as she had always liked mature men who reminded her of her father—men such as Erasmus Wilson, Joaquin Miller, Jules Verne.

They began to talk, freely, naturally, candidly. A sense of well-being came over Nell. She relaxed. It was nice to be in the company of someone wise and understanding and admiring.

In Chicago Nellie Bly and Robert Seaman got off the train together. A few days later on April 5, 1895, they were quietly married there in the Church of the Epiphany.

The *World* carried the story.

"The readers of the Sunday *World* will surely be interested to know that Nellie Bly is married. She is now Mrs. Robert Seaman. Her marriage, like most of the other important events in Nellie Bly's life, was out of the ordinary. She met her husband on the train, on the way to Chicago, only a few days before she became a bride.

"All of the brilliant work of his future bride was well known to Mr. Seaman, and he had, as a regular reader of the *World*, greatly admired Miss Bly. But he had not met her, nor is it likely that he would have contemplated making her his wife if he had not chanced to make her acquaintance."

In a more modest way, the *World* conceded, Mr. Seaman was almost as interesting a person as was Nellie Bly. He had, the paper said, accumulated a fortune of some five million dollars.

"Miss Bly will become the mistress of a metropolitan residence," said the *World*, "a magnificent country seat, a whole stableful of horses, and nearly everything the good fairy of the story books always pictures. Few young women have had more worldly experience than Miss Bly and few are more capable of enjoying the pleasures of a millionaire's existence."

Miss Bly, her paper hastened to add, had been greatly admired by many men, and had had numerous opportunities to wed.

It was natural for people, including the staff of the *World* and business associates of Robert Seaman, to do much speculating about this May-December wedding. Because of its suddenness, and the difference in ages—Seaman was a bachelor of seventy-two—it was assumed by some that Nell had married him for his money. Those who knew her best argued that money for money's sake had never determined Nell's course in the past and that she had not looked for wealthy suitors near her own age. Besides, she herself was earning a fabulous sum.

Then was it a rebound affair, hastily entered into after her broken romance with James Metcalfe? Did she refuse to reach the age of thirty stigmatized by this Victorian age as an "old maid"?

"Yes," said some. "Perhaps,'" said others. "Why did she

do it?" asked the rest. Why had "the darling of the *World*" chosen to marry Robert Seaman?

Nell would have said, if she had said anything, that it was her own personal affair. But, tracing the course of her career, outsiders might have found substantial reasons for her marriage to Robert Seaman.

His background was quite similar to her own. Like Nell, he had worked his way to the top. Like Nell he was tremendously interested in employer-employee relationships.

At the time they met, he had been president and owner of the Ironclad Manufacturing Company in Brooklyn, a large and prosperous hardware concern, for many years. He was also senior director of the Merchants' Exchange National Bank, one of the oldest New York financial institutions. Born in Greene County, New York, in the Catskills, in a colonial house which had been in his family for generations, he was a direct descendant of Dr. Valentine Seaman, the man who first introduced innoculation for smallpox into America.

"The Seamans own property all through and in the vicinity of New York City," said the *World*, "a farm of three hundred acres in the Catskills and other farms in New York State, a sumptuous four-story and basement brownstone mansion at 15 West Thirty-seventh Street, and other realty holdings in Kings, Queens, and Westchester counties."

"Forty years ago," a business associate told a *World* reporter, "Robert Seaman was conspicuous in club life, as it then existed. He was what was then called a beau. He is today one of the most carefully dressed men in New York. In his style, he is rich and quiet, never obtrusive. Should he conclude to entertain in his palatial home on the Hudson or his mansion on Murray Hill, guests will meet a rare gentleman of the Sir Roger de Coverley stamp. His marriage is of course a great surprise to all of us. It would have been at any time during the past twenty years. His associates have always known him as a man of strong convictions and inflexible will.'

As for Nellie Bly, no one knew better than her associates that she was a woman of strong convictions and inflexible will. The *World* carried the old question in regard to their star reporter—What will Nellie Bly do next?

"THE BEST REPORTER IN AMERICA"

NELLIE BLY's departure from the *World* left a void that was never filled. Though sporadic attempts were made to replace her, no other man or woman appeared on the scene with the qualities of mind and personality which made her a phenomenon in newspaper circles.

But if Nell missed the excitement and the thrill of the life she had left behind, there was no indication that her marriage to Robert Seaman was unsuccessful. She accepted the dictates of the Victorian world in which she lived. As the wife of a millionaire, she became a gracious hostess in her beautiful New York residence, entertaining not only her husband's friends and business associates but people from many walks of life. Statesmen came, and reformers, and working girls. Newspaper people, of course, were among her favorite visitors. Erasmus Wilson was a frequent guest, and so was Arthur Brisbane, who had worked with Nell on the *World*.

Robert Seaman and Nell found time for travel, too. Nell's rugged round-the-world jaunt in 1889 had inaugurated improvements in world travel, and they journeyed in comparative luxury.

But it was not in Nell's dynamic nature to remain long on a silken cushion, and she began to take an active part in helping her husband run his business. When he died of a heart attack on March 11, 1904, thirty-seven-year-old Nellie Bly Seaman was left to manage the vast sprawling Brooklyn factory. She threw herself into it with the same determination and energy she had demonstrated in her newspaper days. As president of the Ironclad Manufacturing Company, she worked longer, harder hours than any of her employees. She introduced modern efficiency methods, put up new buildings, drafted and secured the passage in the State Legislature of a law bringing the railroad freight line up to the factory's door. She increased wages and the number of employees, improved working conditions, and created a separate company called the American Steel Barrel Company.

But in 1911, when she attended the funeral of Joseph Pulitzer, financial trouble loomed on the horizon for Nell. In the spring of 1912, expert accountants were called in and found that the company had been robbed by dishonest employees. As the examination continued, it was discovered that hundreds of thousands of dollars were missing.

By the end of 1913, her company was headed for bankruptcy. With prejudice against women in business even stronger than in the newspaper field, Nell found she was fighting a lone battle to prove that women were not misfits there.

In July, 1914, she sailed for Europe. She looked more cheerful than she had in many years as she waved good-by to the friends who saw her off. Still well-groomed and fashionable, she looked like the society woman she had been for years rather than the woman who had waged a bitter fight in business and lost most of her fortune.

"Good-by, Margaret," she called out to Miss Collins, her friend and business associate. "If you want any advice, get in touch with Arthur Brisbane. . . . I'll be back in three weeks."

But she didn't come back in three weeks. Almost immediately, she was caught in the maelstrom of World War I, and found herself interned in Vienna for the duration of the war. It was not until 1919 that she returned to her beloved America.

Almost immediately, she joined the staff of the New York *Evening Journal.* But it is doubtful that Nellie Bly would ever have returned to her "first love" had not financial necessity and the urging of her friend, Arthur Brisbane, prompted her to do so.

Brisbane was now with the *Journal* as a top editorial writer. He knew the tragedy Nell had been through in business; he knew, too, that as the years passed Nell had missed one thing above all else in life—having children of her own. So he proposed she do a column for his paper, using it as a clearing house to find homes for abandoned youngsters.

She responded gladly, joined the *Journal,* and, though she covered other types of stories too in the next several years, found new satisfactions in her work with children.

But it was a strange world to which this older Nellie Bly

returned. Newspapers had changed greatly since her day. There was still prejudice against women on some papers but on others girl reporters were now flocking in, girls who, if they had heard of Nellie Bly at all, knew her only as a legendary figure in newspaper history, a name in some old-fashioned song their mothers used to sing.

Nell saw eager newcomers dash off to assignments, never dreaming that this quiet woman in her small office was the Nellie Bly who had opened the doors of the newspaper world to them and pioneered the work they were now so busy doing; never realizing the reforms she had brought about in America or her impact on its thinking, that even the name Blackwell's Island had been changed to Welfare Island because young Nellie Bly had once passed that way.

And yet this older Nellie Bly covered her last big assignment as bravely and well as she had covered her most famous one, her trip around the world. Although there were no crowds to cheer her photo finish, no buoyant youth and health to sustain her now, she went steadily about the mission of bringing love and bright futures to countless destitute children.

Nor was she through with reform. She brought about the passage of laws for the protection of foster parents who, after giving steadfast devotion to adopted children for years, were often forced by the courts to give these children up on the whims of the real parents who had originally abandoned them. She reunited young couples separated by artificial barriers—parental disapproval, joblessness, creed differences—yet who still wanted to go through life together and share the joys and sorrows of parenthood.

It was during these days on the *Journal* that Nell wrote of her inmost feelings.

"Real love is very rare. What passes for love is generally selfishness. Real love is wholly unselfish. It is something the angels in Heaven might envy."

On the day Nellie Bly became ill with pneumonia, Erasmus Wilson passed away. Ten days later, on January 22, 1922, Nellie Bly, at the age of fifty-four died in St. Mark's Hospital. She was buried from the Church of the Ascension in New York City.

She left no near relatives. There were no blazing headlines to announce that Nellie Bly had started on her last trip, her "travel round the sky." The obituaries were modest ones. But the *Journal* paid her the tribute she would have liked and which she had earned. It said simply, "She was considered the best reporter in America."

APPENDIX

From *The New York Times,* Thursday, February 16, 1956:

Contents of Cornerstone Box of World Building Recall
Earlier Era

BOX YIELDS ITEMS OF PULITZER DAYS

Columbia Journalism School is Heir to 1889 Mementos
from the World Building

❊   ❊   ❊

The World Building has been demolished to make way
for new approaches to the Brooklyn Bridge. The box,
which was laid away on October 10, 1889, was sought
for sixteen months during the wrecking. It fell out of
a mass of brick on February 9.

One historic item in the box was a copy of the *World* of
October 9, 1889. As might be expected, the right-hand
feature column of the front page carried a story by Nellie
Bly. It is a sob sister interview with a convicted Fallen
Woman who slashed her rival. "I held her hand, her lips
trembled. 'Don't forget me. I am deserted. . . . It is so hard
to be alone.' And so with that I took myself away.

(signed) NELLIE BLY."

It could run tomorrow!

MRS. EVA HAMILTON'S STORY.

SHE TALKS FULLY TO "NELLIE BLY" IN TRENTON STATE PRISON.

REMARKABLE STATEMENTS, IF TRUE, OF HER LIFE BEFORE AND AFTER MARRIAGE.

SHE SAYS SHE DIDN'T WANT TO MARRY HAMILTON, AND TELLS WHY.

The First Time She Has Been Able to Speak Freely with a Reporter and to Give Her Side of This Extraordinary Scandal and Romance—How She Met Robert Ray Hamilton, Married Him and Was Blackmailed by "Josh" Mann and His Mother—They Know Her Past Life and Threatened to Tell Her Husband—He Did Not Believe Her Altogether Bad—She Was an Actress for a Year, and for a Time Was with the Florences—Untruths About Her Birth and Childhood—Her Married Life and Her Explanations About Her Baby and the Other Babies—Why She Didn't Tell This Story on Her Trial—Her Diamonds.

[SPECIAL TO THE WORLD.]

TRENTON, N. J., Oct. 8.—I interviewed Mrs.